WHEN TWO PRAY

A Guide for Married Couples

DISCOVER THE POWER
OF PRAYING
AS HUSBAND AND WIFE

"I say unto you, that if two of you shall agree on earth as touching any thing that they shall ask, it shall be done for them of my Father which is in heaven." Matthew 18:19

KAYNEE CORREOSO

To my husband and best friend, Misael,
and for all present and future
Christ-centered households.

TABLE OF CONTENTS

Introduction

FIRST WORDS

My husband and I have been married ten years. Throughout these years we have experienced God's mercy and faithfulness in our lives. However, it was when we started agreeing in prayer that we began to see God work in a powerful way. We have agreed in prayer about many things: the health and salvation of our children, our spiritual growth, guidance in challenging situations, God's strength and wisdom in leading others, among many other petitions.

Yet, the petition that is nearest and dearest to our hearts is that God may use us for the expansion of his kingdom. We want to bring glory to his name by reaching others with the truth of his word so that many may come to know him and surrender to him. We have persevered and agreed in prayer presenting this request before God for many years and every year we have seen God's hand unfolding the response to our prayer in delightfully miraculous ways. So much so that I felt compelled to write this book to tell you just how you and your spouse can experience God's power in your lives through united prayer.

Few spouses consistently implement the collaborative prayer design Jesus advised. It is estimated that between 2% and 8% of Christian couples pray together. That translates into an estimated 92% – 98% of Christian couples that don't come together to pray. Is it any wonder that few couples experience the riches of God's glory and the full extent of his power in their lives?

Jesus himself extends this invitation and promise; "Again I say to you that if two of you agree on earth concerning anything that they ask, it will be done for them by my Father in heaven. For where two or three are gathered together in my name, I am there in the midst of them." (Mt. 18:19-20)

These words are especially meaningful for married couples because only two are necessary to invite God's presence and move his hand in a mighty way. Yes! The power of united prayer with a purpose is insuppressible. This power can be unleashed for your life, your marriage, your family and your highest aspirations for the glory of God and the expansion of his kingdom.

This book will:

       ✳ Enlighten you about the power of prayer when two agree.

✱ Encourage you by demonstrating God's desire for his children to pray and his eagerness to respond.

✱ Teach you and your spouse how to eliminate the most common obstacles for coming together in prayer.

✱ Guide you through questions and discussion points to solidify a life of prayer with your spouse.

✱ Teach you the biblical precursors to answered prayer so you and your spouse may begin experiencing God's power.

✱ Teach you the importance of persistence in prayer.

✱ Explain how to use scripture to effectively pray in alignment with God's will.

⌘ Provide you with key topical scriptures and biblical promises for praying with your spouse.

Each chapter will encourage and enlighten you with biblical passages so that you may successfully come together in prayer and begin experiencing God's abundant miracles in your lives.

I pray the knowledge in this book will bless you and your spouse as it has blessed my husband and me.

Chapter 1

POWER IN UNITY

If Two of You Shall Agree

There is a verse in the bible that is especially powerful for married couples, "Again I say to you that if two of you agree on earth concerning anything that they ask, it will be done for them by my Father in heaven." (Matthew 18:19)

This passage is powerful for you and your spouse because the minimum amount of people required to move God's hand through prayer is merely two. Meaning, you are not required to gather any number of family members or friends to join you in prayer. The number is simply two, "If two of you shall agree."

Agree means to be in one accord, to go together, to have harmony of purpose. Just as musical harmony is generated by the combination of simultaneously sounded notes that produce chords which have a pleasing effect, so the phrase 'harmonious prayer' suggests an ideal agreement of the hearts, souls and minds of those praying to God. When husband and wife come together in purposeful and faithful prayer their offering is like a pleasing melody to the attentive ears of God.

When you and your spouse pray separately, wonderful things happen. God listens and responds. However, when you pray together, the results increase exponentially.

Unity in purpose doesn't just occur by chance; it takes conscientious effort and the investment of time. The ultimate goal in marriage is to consolidate your aspirations, desires, attitudes, and dreams for the glory of God. The intent toward this unity can cause friction and dissidence. Yet, the solution is found in prayer. Praying with your spouse draws you into unity with God and into unity with one another in a significant way.

ANYTHING THEY ASK, SHALL BE DONE

"Anything that they ask, it will be done for them by My Father in heaven." (Matthew 18:19)

Do couples need any more encouragement to pray? Any time and any place husband and wife meet in the name of Jesus trusting in his intercession, they can consider Him as present in their midst, ready to listen and desiring to answer prayers that are in accordance with his will. The question then is: What kind of prayers are in alignment with his will? Prayers that do not come from the natural man but of the born again spiritual man that seeks the glory of God and desires God's will be done on earth as it is in heaven above all things.

We are familiar with a prayer that was void of these terms. "Then the mother of Zebedee's sons came to Him with her sons, kneeling down and asking something from Him. And he said to her, 'What do you wish?' She said to Him, 'Grant that these two sons of mine may sit, one on your right hand and the other on the left, in your kingdom.' But Jesus answered and said, 'You do not know what you ask.'" (Matthew 20:20-22)

This mother's motive was not the glory of God. She sought a prominent position for her two sons. Surely, her motherly love propelled her to make such a petition. However, she was blind to the implications of her request.

On the contrary, when two agree, or have the same focus, purpose, and aspiration to seek the glory of God, live according to his will and consequently articulate prayers that reflect these deeply rooted desires, whatever they ask shall be done for them.

Precursor To Prayer That God Will Answer

What is the nonnegotiable precursor to prayer that God will answer? Jesus himself gives us the answer, "If you abide in me, and my words abide in you, you shall ask what you will, and it shall be done unto you." (John 15:7) When we live in him and his words live in us, our petitions are solidly coordinated and soundly aligned with his will for our lives. Consequently, we ask and receive.

His word abiding in us is simultaneous to God himself abiding in us. "In the beginning was the Word, and the Word was with God, and the Word was God." (John 1:1) The more you and your spouse read, meditate on and study his word the more clearly you will understand God's purpose. Whether you and your spouse are praying for your marriage or others; to support in the delivery of the gospel of truth, for repentance and liberation from sin, for the execution of a miracle, for consolation of the hurting, for the gifts of the Holy Spirit, for the fruit of the spirit, for the revival of those who have strayed away, for a special anointing to convey God's truth to the world or anything else that may be done that is aligned with the glory of God, the purposes of His heart, and the declarations of His will: it shall be done of our Father which is in heaven.

Nothing is impossible for God. He is attentive to the prayer of a single faithful and righteous man; so more of two who agree.

Therefore, pray with your spouse. Pray fervently and persistently with faith and in alignment to the truth of God's words. You will begin to see the miraculous hand of God working in your lives; such as you never thought. Paul understood and experienced God's abundant mercy through answered prayer, "Now unto him that is able to do exceeding abundantly above all that we ask or think, according to the power that works in us." (Ephesians 3:20)

Praying with your spouse invites the presence of God in a greater dimension than praying alone. The prayer of a righteous person is effective and yielding. This is what we learn from the book of James, "The effective, fervent prayer of a righteous man avails much. Elijah was a man with a nature like ours, and he prayed earnestly that it would not rain; and it did not rain on the land for three years and six months. And he prayed again, and the heaven gave rain, and the earth produced its fruit." (James 5:16b-18)

Yet, something unique and exceptional happens when two or more agree in prayer. Let's analyze this truth in detail.

The Effectiveness of United Prayer

Few consistently implement the collaborative prayer design Jesus advised to his disciples. Jesus himself extends this invitation and promise; "Again I say to you that if two of you agree on earth concerning anything that they ask, it will be done for them by My Father in heaven. For where two or three are gathered together in My name, I am there in the midst of them." (Matthew 18:19-20) For every task at hand we would be wise to seek orientation and strength through united prayer. By doing so we highly esteem this precious promise Jesus spoke for us.

Wherever and whenever you and your spouse come together in the name of Jesus, you can know with certainty that he is there with you. His presence is with you when you meet to pray in a beautifully adorned church or a humble cottage, in a field of flowers or the most secluded quarters of an establishment. He is with you when you seek him during the latest hours of the night or when the sun is shining bright. Anywhere and anytime you unite in his name; you can enjoy the privilege of his presence.

The Pulpit Commentary of the bible says it well, "Herein is set forth the privilege of united prayer. God confirms the sentence of his authorized ambassadors; he gives special heed to the joint intercessions of all Christians. Two of you; two of my followers, even the smallest number that could form an association shall agree, be in complete accord, like the notes of a perfect strain of music. Here one man's infirmity is upheld by another's strength; one man's short-sightedness compensated by another's wider view; this man's little faith overpowered by that man's firm confidence."

Yes! As spouses come together for united prayer, one's weakness is compensated by the other's determination. One's limited outlook is compensated by the other's deeply rooted faith. One's disorientation is overpowered by the others purposeful direction. When spouses pray together in the name of Jesus, they are utilizing a magnificent and powerful instrument to support and encourage each other as they surrender to and acknowledge God's sovereignty in their lives. In turn God promises to direct their paths, "Trust in the LORD with all your heart, and lean not on your own understanding; In all your ways acknowledge Him, and He shall direct your paths." (Proverbs 3:5-6)

Peculiar But Glorious Ratio

In Deuteronomy, Moses told the people of Israel, "How could one chase a thousand, and two put ten thousand to flight, unless their rock had sold them, and the Lord had surrendered them?" (Deuteronomy 32:30)

This is a peculiar ratio, isn't it? One to a thousand and two to ten thousand. If the results of what two can accomplish were truly mathematical and equivalent to what one can accomplish, then two would chase two thousand, not ten thousand. However, when two believers come together in Christ there is an exponential increase in the effectiveness of their efforts. If Israel had been wise, they would have defeated all of their enemies with the help of the almighty God; but when they left God, God left them, and therefore they became subjects of their enemies.

The lesson herein is, when husband and wife invite and acknowledge God in everything they do, they become a part of the army with greater strength and power. When we come together with our spouse and invite God in our midst we are making the wisest decision because with him we are *always* on the winning side. Nothing is impossible for God. However, if we should take his power for granted and abandon his invitation to agree in prayer, we pass up the opportunity to experience this illogical but glorious ratio and, much like the people of Israel, run the risk of succumbing to the enemy. Seize the benefits of overcoming the enemy in an overwhelming victory by praying with your spouse!

Reflection Scripture: "Again I say to you that if two of you agree on earth concerning anything that they ask, it will be done for them by my Father in heaven. For where two or three are gathered together in my name, I am there in the midst of them." (Mt. 18:19-20)

Application Time: How can my spouse and I apply the truth of this scripture to our lives?

_____

_____

_____

_____

_____

_____

_____

_____

_____

_____

_____

_____

_____

Chapter 2

ELIMINATING THE OBSTACLES

The Need For United Prayer

It is certain that we are in spiritual warfare. However, while enjoying a picnic at the park on a sunny day, eating out or shopping with a friend one might hardly feel in danger. This spiritual battle, nonetheless, is as real as the sun that rises every morning. Paul puts emphasis on the eminence of this conflict. "For we do not wrestle against flesh and blood, but against principalities, against powers, against the rulers of the darkness of this age, against spiritual hosts of wickedness in the heavenly places." (Ephesians 6:12)

Combat is both difficult and perilous. It is imperative that we prepare for victory! Praying in isolation is similar to fighting a battle alone; no one to strategize with, no one to assist after a fall or a stumble, no one to offer life support via vital and specific requests for assistance. Praying in isolation is neglecting to utilize one of the most potent weapons with exponential power against our enemy.

Paul tells us that our battle isn't against flesh and blood. It is a spiritual conflict. "For though we walk in the flesh, we do not war according to the flesh. For the weapons of our warfare are not carnal but mighty in God for pulling down strongholds, casting down arguments and every high thing that exalts itself against the knowledge of God, bringing every thought into captivity to the obedience of Christ and being ready to punish all disobedience when your obedience is fulfilled." (2 Corinthians10:3-6)

Yes! We are fighting against strongholds, and everything that exalts itself against the knowledge of God. However, we have the power to defeat these things when our obedience is fulfilled. In other words, when we have surrendered to God's will for our lives we have the power to cast down and bind under captivity any spirit of darkness that goes against the wisdom of God.

Prayer is an essential instrument in our spiritual battle. A youth pastor and spiritual leader, learning of the focus and purpose of this book, was eager to share his testimony, "I can attest to praying with your spouse. I think most problems in marriage are caused by demonic influences and our carnality. Praying together can eliminate these influences. My wife and I have been praying together for a few weeks now, and the blessing of God is so evident that it shocked me and has changed her. Yes! I think we are hooked. Now that we are getting used to this awesome blessing over our marriage, we can't go back! It's as if God throws a blanket of peace, love and blessing over us when we pray together. We don't fight. Things just go so well and we have so much love for each other. After experiencing this, I would recommend it to every couple.

Reflection Scripture: "For though we walk in the flesh, we do not war according to the flesh. For the weapons of our warfare are not carnal but mighty in God for pulling down strongholds, casting down arguments and every high thing that exalts itself against the knowledge of God, bringing every thought into captivity to the obedience of Christ and being ready to punish all disobedience when your obedience is fulfilled." (2 Corinthians 10:3-6)

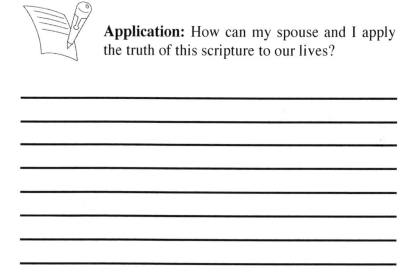

Application: How can my spouse and I apply the truth of this scripture to our lives?

ELIMINATING THE OBSTACLES

Spouses cannot justifiably acquit themselves for
not being all that God intended them to be,
neither can they acquit themselves for not
working together to accomplish God's plan.
No shortcoming can bind us and keep us from
our efforts to live for God and his glory.
No sin can have dominion over us when we call
on the grace of Christ.

"For sin shall not have dominion over you,
for you are not under law but under grace." (Rom. 6:14)

Many couples miss out on abundant and rich
blessings because they do not eliminate the
obstacles associated with being able to
consistently tap into the power of united prayer.
Understand that, whatever the obstacles,
the benefits of praying with your spouse
far out weigh any effort to eliminate them.

This is an invitation to eradicate the barriers and
come before the almighty God with your spouse,
united in heart, spirit and mind.
You'll find a new level of strength and assurance.
You will experience Jesus' transforming power
and the mighty work of the Holy Spirit moving
in your lives.

We will now discuss obstacles that must be eliminated to ensure you can effectively pray on a consistent basis with your spouse.

Confront Your Apprehension

You might be apprehensive about praying with someone, even if it is your spouse. Maybe you are concerned about the 'appropriate' articulation of your prayers or the vulnerability that comes with praying while someone else listens.

If this is the case, begin by praying aloud when you are alone. Pray aloud as you're driving down the road on your way to work and back. Pray aloud as you are folding laundry or working on the car. Speak to God with sincerity, reverence and faith. Pray with a broken and contrite heart. This is the only formula for a pristinely composed prayer. "The sacrifices of God are a broken spirit, a broken and a contrite heart. These, O God, you will not despise." (Psalm 51:17) Let God know of your gratitude, your deepest desires, your worries and your fears. "Casting all your care upon Him, for He cares for you." (1 Peter 5:7) Speak to your father in heaven confidently about your aspirations to do his will and bring glory to his name. Ask him for a shield of protection around you and your family. Give him your adoration and praise. Do this aloud and rejoice in this practice on a daily basis.

You will consequently find that praying audibly with your spouse becomes a non-threatening practice. When you pray together, you will pray with confidence because of your familiarity with this sincere communication with God stemming from your personal relationship with Him.

As an added benefit, due to the sense of vulnerability in shared prayer, because you are voicing your worries and fears before your spouse, you will also experience a deeper understanding of each other's hearts and greater depth in your relationship. Praying together is a sign of great trust. Being unguarded on your own before God is a fulfilling experience. Yet, being vulnerable before your spouse will strengthen your bond and friendship. You will soon find that this time together is the most gratifying time of your day and God's greatest gift to your marriage.

 Questions/Discussion Starters
To complete with your spouse for
the purpose of generating actionable steps.

1. Are there fears inhibiting you from coming to the Lord together in prayer? If so, present them to your spouse. Speak openly about your fears, brainstorm solutions and pray for overcoming them.

_____

_____

_____

_____

_____

_____

2. Recite this verse together, "For God has not given us a spirit of fear, but of power and of love and of a sound mind." (2 Timothy 1:7) Jot down what this scripture means for you.

_____

_____

_____

_____

3. Talk about what would help to make this time of prayer a pleasurable experience. Create a plan below.

_____

_____

_____

_____

_____

_____

_____

_____

_____

_____

_____

Making The Time

Finding time to pray in an already busy schedule will take intentional planning. Hoping to make time for prayer is not an effective strategy. You must strategically make prayer a priority.

Make an appointment to pray just like you would for any other commitment of importance. Make this engagement before or after something you do on a daily basis so that it is easily integrated into your daily routine. This may be right after you and your spouse get out of bed in the morning, in the evening after dinner, after putting the kids to bed or before retiring for the night. Be purposeful. Put the appointment on your calendar and make that time sacred. If you have children and they are present during this time it is both valuable and instructive for them to see you praying together. Invite them to join you. This will advance them into the discipline of prayer and will significantly impact their reliance on an almighty God. No matter when you pray, this time will be the most effective medicine to deepen your relationship with God, despite a hectic schedule.

If you've agreed on the daily time you and your spouse will set aside for prayer, and you are concerned about your own endless occupations during the day that impede you from coming to God individually in prayer, pray about this with your spouse. Pray that God may put his hand over your daily schedules so that you may keep your individual conversations with God going throughout the day.

Remember that knowing God and his son Jesus Christ through an intimate relationship is eternal life, "And this is eternal life, that they may know you, the only true God, and Jesus Christ whom you have sent." (John 17:3)

Questions/Discussion Starters
To complete with your spouse for
the purpose of generating actionable steps.

1. Consult your calendars and agree on your time of prayer. Book this time on your schedules and make this time sacred.

_____

_____

_____

_____

_____

2. Discuss the location where you will pray. Will you have a designated spot for prayer? Or will you pray right where you are when it is time to pray?

_____

_____

_____

_____

_____

3. Agree on the amount of time you would like to dedicate to prayer.

_____

_____

_____

_____

_____

4. Secure a journal to record your prayer requests or write them below. When God answers, check these requests off and give him praise. These answered prayers will augment your faith. Then together testify of the things God has done.

_____

_____

_____

_____

_____

_____

_____

_____

_____

_____

One More Thing

Avoid the danger of viewing this time of prayer as 'one more thing'. Don't come before God as another thing to check off your to-do-list. Enjoy this special time with God. Shift your mentality from *having to* spend time with God, to *having the delightful privilege* of spending time with God. Assuredly, there is fullness of joy in his presence. "You will show me the path of life; In your presence is fullness of joy; At your right hand are pleasures forevermore." (Psalm 16:11)

There may be days when you will not meet the engagement of praying with your spouse. If that happens, forgive yourself and reassume this time of prayer the following day. Always remember the benefits prayer brings. Prayer will succeed where other measures have been unsuccessful. Praying with your spouse should not be your last resort or a reactive measure when all else has failed. Praying together should be your *first response*. Setting aside time for prayer has the power to change every other part of your day and transform your lives.

Remember Jeremiah 29:11-13 has a powerful promise for those who call upon him and seek him with all their heart. " 'For I know the plans I have for you,' declares the LORD, 'plans to prosper you and not to harm you, plans to give you hope and a future. Then you will call upon me and come and pray to me, and I will listen to you. You will seek me and find me when you seek me with all your heart.' "

Questions/Discussion Starters
To complete with your spouse for
the purpose of generating actionable steps.

1. Think about what would make this time of devotion wholesomely enjoyable. Jot down your ideas below.

_____

_____

_____

_____

_____

2. Would you like to integrate a time of praise and worship? Delineate this time below.

_____

_____

_____

_____

_____

_____

_____

3. See chapters 6, 7 and 8 to learn how to pray scripture and for topical scriptures and biblical promises to pray with your spouse.

4. If you do not own a study bible, acquire one for each of you. Generate a study plan below or research a bible study plan that you can both follow to grow in the knowledge of God as you meditate on his word. Carefully study each passage, highlight important parts and make notes about how you and your spouse will apply each passage to your lives.

_____

_____

_____

_____

_____

_____

_____

_____

_____

_____

_____

_____

_____

_____

5. Make notes about God's promises. Pray these promises and thank God for his faithfulness in keeping his promises.

God's promises for us: (See chapter 8)

_____

_____

_____

_____

_____

_____

_____

_____

_____

_____

_____

_____

_____

_____

_____

_____

_____

_____

About Face: Confessing and Abandoning Sin

"Now we know that God does not hear sinners; but if anyone is a worshiper of God and does his will, he hears him." (John 9:31)

God is three times holy. We are not. However, we are reconciled with him through the blood of Jesus Christ. This reconciliation comes with repentance and the renouncing of sin. If you or your spouse are living in sin, or if both of you are under the bondage of sin, repentance and forsaking of sin is necessary when coming before the throne of grace. "If I regard iniquity in my heart, The Lord will not hear." (Psalms 66:18)   This specifically refers to recurring, deliberate and conscientious acts of sin.

Anything that takes God's place is sin for us. This could be material possessions, a hobby, our bodies, a relationship a career or a certain role or position. It is God who we must love with all our heart, soul, mind and strength. Knowing and loving him is our priority. "And you shall love the Lord your God with all your heart, with all your soul, with all your mind, and with all your strength.' This *is* the first commandment." (Mark 12:30)

What is taking God's place in your spouse's life or your life? We must cut all ties to the weight of earthly things that take God's place.

"I once heard of two men who, under the influence of liquor, came down one night to where their boat was tied; they wanted to return home, so they got in and began to row. When the grey dawn of morning broke, behold, they had never loosed the mooring line, or raised the anchor. And that's just the way with many who are striving to enter the kingdom of heaven. They cannot believe, because they are tied to this world. Cut the cord! Cut the cord! Set yourselves free from the clogging weight of earthly things." - D.L. Moody

Repentance implies forsaking sin, making an about face, getting in a different lane and going in the opposite direction. It is making a U-turn, taking a different route, jumping on another train, letting go of the chains and accepting freedom.

"If you abide in my word, you are My disciples indeed. And you shall know the truth, and the truth shall make you *free*." John 8:31-32

Moody explains, "If you want to be converted, and want to repent, I will tell you what you should do. Just get out of Satan's service, and get into the Lord's. Leave your old friends, and unite yourself with God's people. I shall be gone on a journey shortly. If, when I am in the train, a friend should say, "Moody, you are going in the wrong train." "My friend," I should say, "you have made a great mistake; the guard told me this is the right train. You are wrong, I am sure you are wrong. The guard told me this is the right train." Then my friend would say, "Moody, I have lived here forty years, and I know all about the trains. That train is the wrong one." He at last convinces me, and I get out of that train and get into the right one. Repentance is getting out of one train and getting into the other. You are on the wrong train; you are in the broad path that takes you down to the pit of hell. Get out of it tonight. Right about face! Who will turn his feet towards God? "Turn ye, for why will ye die?" In the Old Testament the word is 'turn.' In the New Testament the word is 'repent.' "

Husbands and wives, make an about face. If there are sins that must be forgiven, tell God in prayer that you repent and abandon your sin. He will mold you and lead your life and marriage to become everything he intended it to be. "If my people who are called by my name will humble themselves, and pray and seek my face, and turn from their wicked ways, then I will hear from heaven, and will forgive their sin and heal their land." (2 Chronicles 7:14)

Questions/Discussion Starters
To complete with your spouse for
the purpose of generating actionable steps.

1. Remember that no sin can have dominion over you when you call on the grace of Christ. Are there sins that you need to confess?

_____

_____

_____

_____

_____

_____

_____

_____

2. Repentance implies forsaking sin, making an about face, getting in a different lane and going in the opposite direction. What must be radically removed or changed in your life so that you can forsake your sins?

_____

_____

_____

_____

_____

3. Are there disagreements between you and your spouse about whether a certain action is a sin? If so, what does the bible say? Study the word of God together. In it you will find the truth that will set you free.

_____

_____

_____

_____

_____

_____

_____

_____

_____

_____

Husbands and Hindered Prayers

Peter tells husbands how to live with their wives so that their prayers will not be hindered.

"Husbands, likewise, dwell with them with understanding, giving honor to the wife, as to the weaker vessel, and as being heirs together of the grace of life, that your prayers may not be hindered." (1 Peter 3:7)

Husbands, if you would like your prayers to be lifted before the throne of God you must know there is a specific way to treat your wife. You honor your wife when you make an intentional effort to understand her on a deeper level and meet her needs with love. You must esteem her, value her and recognize her. Know that she is the weaker vessel. She needs you to be the spiritual leader of the family. Peter's teaches that she, too, is an heir of the grace of life.

When husbands treat their wives with understanding, honor and affability their prayers aren't hindered. On the contrary, they are helped or brought forth to God.

Bitterness, resentment and rancor between spouses is an impediment to forgiveness through prayer. It is natural for the flesh to plot revenge, to lash back or to avoid the offender when there are hurt feelings and discontentment. However, God requires forgiveness. If we don't forgive, he will not forgive us. "And whenever you stand praying, if you have anything against anyone, forgive him, that your Father in heaven may also forgive you your trespasses." (Mark 11:25)

If spouses do not bear and forgive each other, there is no use in coming to God in prayer for the forgiveness of sins because God will forgive our sins, as we forgive our debtors. (Matthew 6:12)

Questions/Discussion Starters
To complete with your spouse for
the purpose of generating actionable steps.

1. Is there bitterness, resentment or rancor in your relationship? If so, respectfully talk about what has hurt you. Put your feelings out in the open without accusing or utilizing 'you' statements. Instead begin your statements with 'I'. Ex. *I felt demeaned and belittled by your words.*

_____

_____

_____

_____

_____

_____

_____

_____

_____

2. Seek first to understand. When both of you have exchanged your thoughts and heart, apologize. Say, 'I'm sorry' or ask, 'Will you forgive me?' or restitute with 'I would like to make this up to you by …'

_____

_____

_____

_____

_____

_____

_____

_____

_____

_____

_____

_____

_____

3. Forgive so that Christ will forgive you.

4. Pray so that God will help you leave past offenses in the past.

We Must Pray While Living Faithfully

Our sins separate us from God. "Behold, the Lord's hand is not shortened, that it cannot save; nor His ear heavy, that it cannot hear. But your iniquities have separated you from your God; and your sins have hidden *His* face from you, so that He will not hear." (Isaiah 59:1-2)

Before Jesus died on the cross there was a great divide between God and man. To receive forgiveness of sins a priest had to offer a sacrifice on an altar. The blood of this sacrificial lamb served as atonement for sin. Nonetheless, man was in a never-ending cycle of perdition; sin, sacrifice, sin, sacrifice, sin... you get the picture. However, the good news of the gospel is: Jesus' blood shed on the cross paid the price once and for all! His blood cleanses us from our past, present and future sins. The price is paid! All we must do is believe in the power of his blood and come to him in faith and repentance. Then the Lord will hear our prayers and forgive our sins. Yet, if we esteem and harbor sinfulness in our hearts, God will not listen to our prayers. "If I regard iniquity in my heart, the Lord will not hear." (Psalm 66:18)

God rejects the prayers of the impenitent. Too many people live their lives for their own desires and then go racing to God in time of need. They expect God to answer them despite the fact they refuse to serve him and abide by his commandments. The word of God says this will not work. "One who turns away his ear from hearing the law, even his prayer *is* an abomination." (Proverbs 28:9)

God's desire for us is our sanctification. He does not want us returning to 'square one' engaging in the same sins repeatedly. He desires our conscientious and consistent effort toward spiritual growth. This demonstrates sincere repentance. Repentance is evidenced when we desire and live to do only what is pleasing to God. Then we shall ask and receive from Him. "Beloved, if our heart does not condemn us, we have confidence toward God and whatever we ask we receive from Him, because we keep His commandments and do those things that are pleasing in His sight." (1 John 3:21-22)

Husbands and wives, do you want God to listen to and respond to your prayers? Repent of your sins and live in obedience to Him. Ensure you are of the righteous and not of those who do evil. "For the eyes of the Lord *are* on the righteous, and His ears *are open* to their prayers; but the face of the Lord *is* against those who do evil." (1 Peter 3:12)

Truly, "The Lord *is* far from the wicked, but He hears the prayer of the righteous." (Proverbs 15: 29) Commit to living faithfully. Commit to sanctifying your lives and your marriage for the glory of God.

Questions/Discussion Starters
To complete with your spouse for
the purpose of generating actionable steps.

1. Are you and your spouse willing, whether approved or disapproved by others and the standard 'norm' of this world, to hold firmly to the true Biblical teachings of God and the life of integrity, love and justice Christ demonstrated and taught? What are these 'standard norms' and how can you hold firmly to the truth of God's word.

_____

_____

_____

_____

_____

_____

_____

_____

_____

_____

_____

_____

_____

_____

2. Is there a particular sin that you continue to engage in despite having repented of it numerous times in the past? What steps must you take to abandon this sin completely? What would going in the opposite direction of this sin look like, sound like, feel like?

_____

_____

_____

_____

_____

_____

_____

_____

3. Write down any sin(s) you would like to eradicate from your life. Is there anything you need to remove or take away from your home or abandon in the form of habits or friendships to ensure that there is no room for further temptation? If so, act on this removal or abandonment now.

_____

_____

_____

_____

_____

_____

4. Next to each sin you would like to eradicate, write down the righteous act you'd like to replace that sin should you feel the temptation to engage in it again. Ask God to give you the strength through Jesus Christ to live a life of righteousness. "I can do all things through Christ who strengthens me." (Philippians 4:13)

_____

_____

_____

_____

_____

_____

_____

_____

_____

5. Together with your spouse, celebrate freedom from crippling desires and disobedience to God's perfect will for your lives. Remember, "Do not be conformed to this world, but be transformed by the renewing of your mind, that you may prove what is that good and acceptable and perfect will of God." Romans 12:2

_____

_____

_____

_____

My Spouse Won't Pray With Me

Invite your spouse to pray. However, if your invitation is not well received despite numerous and varied attempts, rather than seeking to force your spouse into united prayer, engage in other disciplines that allow you to grow closer to God and know Him on a more intimate level. We should *never* give up on prayer. However, there are other ways couples can grow in their relationship with God that will lead to an open door for united prayer in the future.

Spiritual intimacy is about having closeness with God and knowing Him. Let's look at a couple of spiritual disciplines in which couples can participate to know God more intimately and receive wisdom and direction from Him.

Attend church together

Hebrews 10: 24-25 commands every Christian to be a part of a body of believers and tells us why this is necessary.

"And let us consider one another in order to stir up love and good works, not forsaking the assembling of ourselves together, as *is* the manner of some, but exhorting *one another,* and so much the more as you see the day approaching." (Hebrews 10: 24-25)

It is only in the church that we can find the level of affinity that is required to consider one another to stir up "love and good deeds." This is the prime setting to encourage and support one another as we learn about and model after the love of God.

Also, when Paul gave Timothy direction in regards to public meetings, he said, "Till I come, give attention to reading, to exhortation, to doctrine." (1Timothy 4:13). Coming together in worship includes: Growing in the knowledge of God through reading and hearing his word and being called to obedience through exhortation. It is in the context of the local church that these things occur.

Likewise, couples who attend church will learn to consider one another with love and good deeds and will grow in the knowledge of God by the admonition of his word. These things occur through the intercession of the Holy Spirit.

Read the bible together

The family unit was established by God. Therefore, Satan hates families. He knows that if he can destroy the family, he will destroy the church and eventually the community and the nation. He is constantly pursuing to destroy families by splitting up it's members through the works of the flesh. Satan works hard to keep husbands and wives away from the word of God. He doesn't want us to read and understand the Words of Life that unmask his lies and bring knowledge of eternal truth and life. Satan asked Eve, "Has God said?" Neither Adam nor Eve were deeply convicted of what God had commanded. Therefore, they easily succumbed to Satan's lies. For this reason, it is important to remember that you can never elevate your spouse above the level of your own intimacy with God.

Society puts great emphasis on sexual performance…but the real question is: How are you and your spouse performing spiritually? The invitation for spiritual growth is for you and your spouse today.

So, grow in the grace and knowledge of Jesus Christ through reading and studying the word of God. Don't point an accusatory finger at your spouse; rather, hold each other by the hand and enjoy a time of spiritual intimacy with God by reading his word together. The discipline of united prayer will come as a consequence of your spiritual growth.

Persevere With Patience

Although the afore mentioned disciplines do not replace prayer, they are essential for spiritual growth and intimacy with God. Patiently persevere in going to church and reading the word with your spouse. This will enable you to connect with each other as you grow in your connection with God. United prayer will come as a product of the intimacy that develops from these disciplines.

 Questions/Discussion Starters
To complete together with your spouse for the purpose of generating actionable steps.

1. Is there a lack of spiritual growth keeping you from coming to the Lord together in prayer? If so, engage in the disciplines described above together. Do so even when initially they may not seem desirable. Pray individually for your spiritual growth and for that of your spouse.

2. Spiritual growth entails: (1) increasing in your knowledge of the word of God (2) decreasing the frequency of sin, (3) increasing in a Christ-like character, and (4) increasing in your faith in God. The best overview of spiritual growth is becoming like Jesus Christ. In 1 Corinthians 11:1 Paul says, "Imitate me, just as I also *imitate* Christ."

_____

_____

_____

_____

_____

3. Is there bitterness or resentment in your relationship keeping you from wanting to come together in prayer? If so, respectfully talk about what has hurt you. Forgive each other as God forgives you.

_____

_____

_____

_____

_____

_____

_____

4. Are there sins that either of you need to confess that are distancing you from God? What must be radically removed or changed in your life so that you can forsake these sins?

_____

_____

_____

_____

_____

_____

_____

_____

_____

_____

_____

_____

_____

_____

Chapter 3

ENCOURAGEMENT FOR PRAYER

It Shall Be Done!

The power of united prayer with a purpose is insuppressible. This power can be unleashed for your life, your marriage, your family and your highest aspirations for the glory of God and the expansion of his kingdom.

"Prayer has already divided seas and rolled up flowing rivers, it has made flinty rocks gush into fountains, it has quenched flames of fire, it has muzzled lions, disarmed vipers and poisons, it has marshaled the stars against the wicked, it has stopped the course of the moon and arrested the sun in its race, it has burst open iron gates and recalled souls from eternity, it has conquered the strongest devils and commanded legions of angels down from heaven. Prayer has bridled and chained the raging passions of men and destroyed vast armies of proud, daring, blustering atheists. Prayer has brought one man from the bottom of the sea and carried another in a chariot of fire to heaven." - Anonymous

Is there anything that God cannot do when we pray according to his purpose? Assuredly, he is powerful and mighty. Absolutely *everything* is possible for him.

The prophet Jeremiah understood the omnipotence of God. He heard the voice of the Lord telling him that he knew him before he formed him in his mother's womb. He evidenced the power of God when he sent him forth as a prophet to the nations. God himself touched Jeremiah's lips and put His words in his mouth. The Lord commanded and Jeremiah spoke. He promised to deliver Jeremiah from his enemies and he did. Jeremiah experienced, first hand, every one of these humbling and mighty acts of God. Hence, it is understandable why he would exclaim, "Ah, Lord GOD! Behold, you have made the heavens and the earth by your great power and outstretched arm. There is nothing too hard for you." (Jeremiah 32:17)

God's power and authority have no limits. Therefore, when your prayers are uncorrupted petitions that are distinctly aligned with his will, God says, "It shall be done!" There is great satisfaction in this, isn't there? It shall be done!

Why is it that praying on the basis of the *will* and the *glory of God* can move God's hand in such a mighty way? Simply because we were created to fulfill his will for his glory. God has a perfect plan for your life that in his loving kindness *he wants to fulfill*. The will of God is described by the apostle Paul as '*good* and *perfect*'. However, God will not force his will upon you. We are to desire this *good* and *perfect* will because we've understood how gratifying and wonderful it is for us and how it in turn brings glory to his name. We are to seek and pursue his will and learn to love it through an intimate relationship with him.

Therefore, when praying with your spouse, part from the perfect will of God. This is the foundation to prayer that is like a delicate perfume to God. "Now this is the confidence that we have in him, that if we ask anything according to his will, he hears us. And if we know that he hears us, whatever we ask, we know that we have the petitions that we have asked of him." (1 John 5:14-15) His desires should be our desires. His will should be our will. This is the spirit in the Lord's Prayer, "Your kingdom come, your will be done on earth as it is in heaven." (Matthew 6:10) This is the spirit we want guiding our every prayer.

Nonetheless, honestly praying in alignment with God's will only comes when the Holy Spirit is actively working in our lives. When this is the case, the Holy Spirit intercedes for us in prayer. "Likewise the Spirit also helps in our weaknesses. For we do not know what we should pray for as we ought, but the Spirit Himself makes intercession for us with groanings which cannot be uttered. Now He who searches the hearts knows what the mind of the Spirit is, because He makes intercession for the saints according to the will of God." (Romans 8:26-27) How glorious that we should have the Holy Spirit to teach us and guide us in our most intimate conversations with God!

Isaiah spoke to Israel and gave them the promise of God, "It shall come to pass that before they call, *I will answer*; and while they are still speaking, *I will hear*." (Isaiah 65:24)

This is a promise from God not only for the people of Israel, but for us, as well.

There is great delight in this, isn't there? I will hear! I will answer!

Christ's Intercession in Prayer

Let's discuss the following two versus and what they mean. "Whatever you ask in my name, that I will do, that the Father may be glorified in the Son. If you ask anything in my name, I will do it." (John 14:13-14) "In Jesus name" is not a magic formula. We don't disclose this phrase at the end of our prayers so that God may grant our every desire. To pray in Jesus' name is to pray with the intercession of Jesus. To pray in the name of Jesus is to pray for God's will to be done on earth as it is in heaven just as it was done through Jesus when he walked on earth. We pray in Jesus' name because his blood allows us to come before the throne of God anytime, anywhere.

D.L. Moody once retold a conversation he had with a certain man, "Not long ago a man said to me, "I cannot believe." "Whom?" I asked. He stammered, and again said, "I cannot believe." I said, "Whom?" "Well," he said, "I can't believe." "Whom?" I asked again. At last he said, "I cannot believe myself." "Well, you don't need to. You do not need to put any confidence in yourself. The less you believe in yourself the better." "

When we trust in Jesus' strength and not our own, we begin to see unimaginable miracles performed in our lives. This is because when we surrender to him, he works in everything, including our will and actions, according to his desire. "For it is God who works in you both *to will* and *to do* for his good pleasure." (Philippians 2:13)

Knowing this to be true, this morning my husband and I prayed, "Father we want to work for you, for your glory, for the expansion of your kingdom. We know we cannot do this on our own. We give ourselves to you. We ask that you use our minds, our mouths and hands to do your work. Just as Elisha, give us a double portion of your Holy Spirit so that we may overcome any obstacle. Do the same work in us as you did in your disciples. They went from hiding in fear to evangelizing for the conversion of thousands across many lands. This was done through the power of your Holy Spirit. We know you said that without you we can do nothing. We surrender our lives to you. We believe we can do all things through Christ who strengthens us! In the name of Jesus we pray. Amen."

Yes! We cannot do anything of eternal value without Him. We can attempt it. However, we will end up just like branches that have been broken from a tree: lifeless, hollow, dry and good for casting into the fire. Jesus taught us this when he said, "I am the vine, you are the branches. He who abides in me, and I in him, bears much fruit; for without Me you can do nothing" (John 15:5b)

What exactly does it mean to abide in Jesus?

We abide in Jesus when we know him. When we allow him to speak to us through his word. When we enter into an intimate relationship with him through prayer. We abide in him when he speaks to our hearts and we listen and obey. We then begin bearing fruit because we are deeply rooted in him. Noticing the growth of his fruit in our lives augments our faith and we in turn seek him with greater confidence and conviction because we understand, from experience, that the closer we grow to him the more his wondrous grace will work in us. So thus continues a glorious cycle that is the gift that keeps on giving. We then fully understand Paul's words to the Ephesians, "... what is the exceeding greatness of His power toward us who believe, according to the working of His mighty power which He worked in Christ when He raised Him from the dead and seated Him at His right hand in the heavenly places." (Ephesians 1:19-20) The same power that worked in Jesus when he was raised from the dead is the power that works in us.

I rejoice in the manner R.A. Torrey describes abiding in Christ:

"...to abide in Christ is to renounce any independent life of our own, to give up trying to think our thoughts, or form our resolutions, or cultivate our feelings, and simply and constantly look to Christ to think his thoughts in us, to form his purposes in us, to feel his emotions and affections in us. It is to renounce all life independent of Christ, and constantly to look to him for the inflow of his life into us, and the outworking of his life through us. When we do this, and in so far as we do this, our prayers will obtain that which we seek from God. This must necessarily be so, for our desires will not be our own desires, but Christ's, and our prayers will not in reality be our own prayers, but Christ praying in us. Such prayers will always be in harmony with God's will, and the Father hears them always. When our prayers fail it is because they are indeed our prayers. We have conceived the desire and framed the petition of ourselves, instead of looking to Christ to pray through us. To say that one should be abiding in Christ in all his prayers, looking to Christ to pray through him rather than praying himself, is simply saying in another way that one should pray "in the Spirit." When we thus abide in Christ, our thoughts are not our own thoughts, but his, our joys are not our own joys, but his, our fruit is not our own fruit, but his; just as the buds, leaves, blossoms and fruit of the branch that abides in the vine are not the buds, leaves, blossoms and fruit of the branch, but of the vine itself whose life is flowing into the branch and manifests itself in these buds, leaves, blossoms and fruit."

Glory in that! Rejoice in the fact that Jesus lives and moves within you and your spouse when you abide in him. Celebrate and give thanks that your lives belong to him and that his will is done in you. Delight in the fact that your prayers are answered by his merit and in his name!

What Can Spouses Learn From The Early Church?

The early church realized the power of united prayer. The bible tells us they gathered to pray for boldness after the Sanhedrin persecuted them. Luke explains the sequence of events like this, "And being let go, they went to their own companions and reported all that the chief priests and elders had said to them. So when they heard that, they raised their voice to God with one accord and said: 'Lord, you are God, who made heaven and earth and the sea, and all that is in them, who by the mouth of your servant David have said: 'Why did the nations rage, and the people plot vain things? The kings of the earth took their stand, and the rulers were gathered together against the Lord and against His Christ. For truly against your holy Servant Jesus, whom you anointed, both Herod and Pontius Pilate, with the Gentiles and the people of Israel, were gathered together to do whatever your hand and your purpose determined before to be done. Now, Lord, look on their threats, and grant to your servants that with all boldness they may speak your word, by stretching out your hand to heal, and that signs and wonders may be done through the name of your holy Servant Jesus.' And when they had prayed, the place where they were assembled together was shaken; and they were all filled with the Holy Spirit, and they spoke the word of God with boldness." (Acts 4:23-31)

Here we see an immediate response to prayer. The place where the early church was gathered shook and they were filled with the Holy Spirit. Furthermore, they were granted the boldness they had requested to speak the word of God with inextinguishable courage. Never again do we see the apostles hiding in fear. "And with great power the apostles gave witness to the resurrection of the Lord Jesus and great grace was upon them all." (Acts 4:33) They valiantly preached the gospel to those around them with great power, often times out in plain sight where every ear could hear the good news.

In Acts chapter 12 we learn of another instance in which the church came together to pray and their petition was granted immediately. In this instance the church gathered to pray in the house of Mary, John's mother. They prayed for Peter who at the time was incarcerated.

From the following passage we can see that God's response was prompt and astonishing to those gathered in prayer. "Peter was therefore kept in prison, but constant prayer was offered to God for him by the church. And when Herod was about to bring him out, that night Peter was sleeping, bound with two chains between two soldiers; and the guards before the door were keeping the prison. Now behold, an angel of the Lord stood by him, and a light shone in the prison; and he struck Peter on the side and raised him up, saying, "Arise quickly!" And his chains fell off his hands … So he went out and followed him, and did not know that what was done by the angel was real, but thought he was seeing a vision. When they were past the first and the second guard posts, they came to the iron gate that leads to the city, which opened to them of its own accord; and they went out and went down one street, and immediately the angel departed from him." (Acts 12:5-10)

When this occurred Peter went to Mary's house and knocked on the door. Those praying could not believe that it was Peter standing at the gate. In this passage we can see the astonished response of those who prayed for Peter's liberation, "He (Peter) came to the house of Mary … where many were gathered together praying. And as Peter knocked at the door of the gate, a girl named Rhoda came to answer. When she recognized Peter's voice, because of her gladness she did not open the gate, but ran in and announced that Peter stood before the gate. But they said to her, 'You are beside yourself!' Yet, she kept insisting that it was so. So they said, 'It is his angel.' Now Peter continued knocking;

and when they opened the door and saw him, they were *astonished*. But motioning to them with his hand to keep silent, he declared to them how the Lord had brought him out of the prison." (Acts 12:12-17a)

Likewise, when you and your spouse, as members of the body of Christ, agree and pray in accordance with the purposes of God, you will find yourselves, just like the early church who prayed for Peter, astonished and amazed at the power of God manifested. You will find God's answers to your prayers are, "...abundantly above all that we ask or think, according to the power that works in us." (Ephesians 3:20)

If You Ever Get Discouraged

If you and your spouse ever get discouraged in prayer, if you ever have a need to pray ardently and eagerly but have a hard time overcoming hopelessness because of unanswered prayers, remember that God has not forgotten you.

Many times God responds promptly after we come to Him in prayer. Other times he responds after much asking and seeking. Yet, other times he doesn't respond at all because our prayers were not in accordance with his will. Remember that God's goal is not to grant our every request. His goal is to make us sanctified vessels that are set aside and prepared for every good work for his glory. "But in a great house there are not only vessels of gold and silver, but also of wood and clay, some for honor and some for dishonor. Therefore if anyone cleanses himself from the latter, he will be a vessel for honor, sanctified and useful for the Master, prepared for every good work." (2 Timothy

2:20-21) Therefore, if God has not responded, rejoice in the fact that he is using your current situation to change you, to sanctify you for his glory. Thank God in prayer. Present him a heart filled with gratitude for he has already done a wondrous work by saving us from the wrath of his justice through Jesus and he continually molds us through every situation to make us what we ought to be.

Furthermore, continue to claim God's promises through prayer. Persist in prayer because there is a great reward for those who do. God's attributes and love far transcend any alternate source we might go to for help. He, this all-knowing and powerful God, invites us to persist in prayer. So, do. Persevere. Don't give up! Continue to ask, seek and knock. God is in control and when the time is right he will respond. He is never late. God is always right on time.

SEIZE GOD'S PROMISES

God spoke many promises to encourage us in prayer. The story of Mithridates, a celebrated king in Asia and an old musician, illustrates the many riches that are already ours in His promises.

"This king became interested in an old musician who had taken part in the music performed at a feast in the royal palace. On awaking one morning, this old man saw the tables in his house covered with vessels of silver and gold; a number of servants were standing by, who offered him rich garments to put on, and told him there was a horse standing at the door for his use, whenever he might wish to ride. The old man thought it was only a dream he was having. But the servants said it was no dream at all. It was reality. 'What is the meaning of it?' asked the astonished old man. 'It means this,' said the servant, 'the king has determined to make you a rich man at once. And these things that you see are only a small part of what he has given you. So please use them as your own.' At last he believed what they told him. Then he put on the purple robe, and mounted the horse; and as he rode along, he kept saying to himself, 'All these are mine! All these are mine!'" - D.L. Moody

You and your spouse do the same. Seize these promises, claim them by saying, "All these are ours! All these are ours!" Many people read and contemplate these promises in unbelief much like the old musician did initially with the riches shown to him. They don't believe these promises can be for them. Therefore, they don't reach out in faith through prayer to claim them. God's desire to listen and respond to our prayers is evident in each of the scriptures that follow. Consequently, we find ample encouragement in them.

 Reflection Scriptures: If you ever get discouraged, read through these scriptures with your spouse.

"And this is the confidence that we have in him, that, if we ask any thing according to his will, he heareth us: And if we know that he hears us, whatsoever we ask, we know that we have the petitions that we desired of him." (1 John 5:14-15)

"For there is no difference between the Jew and the Greek: for the same Lord over all is rich unto all that call upon him." (Romans 10:12)

"Let us therefore come boldly unto the throne of grace, that we may obtain mercy, and find grace to help in time of need." (Hebrews 4:16)

"Ask, and it shall be given you; seek, and ye shall find; knock, and it shall be opened unto you." (Matthew 7:7)

"Again I say unto you, That if two of you shall agree on earth as touching any thing that they shall ask, it shall be done for them of my Father which is in heaven." (Matthew 18:19)

"And all things, whatsoever ye shall ask in prayer, believing, ye shall receive." (Matthew 21:22)

"Therefore I say unto you, what things so ever ye desire, when ye pray, believe that ye receive them, and ye shall have them." (Mark 11:24)

"If ye then, being evil, know how to give good gifts unto your children: how much more shall your heavenly Father give the Holy Spirit to them that ask him?" (Luke 11:13)

"And whatsoever ye shall ask in my name, that will I do, that the Father may be glorified in the Son. If ye shall ask any thing in my name, I will do it." (John 14:13-14)

"And in that day ye shall ask me nothing. Verily, verily, I say unto you, whatsoever ye shall ask the Father in my name, he will give it you." (John 16:23)

Chapter 4

PRECURSORS TO ANSWERED PRAYERS

We Must Pray In Accordance With God's Will

God wants us to come to him in prayer. However, there are conditions we must meet in order for God to hear and answer us.

Spouses may come confidently before the throne of God when asking for anything that is in accordance to God's will. "Now this is the confidence that we have in Him, that if we ask anything according to his will, he hears us." (1 John 5:14-15) We learn about his will for our lives and come to know him more intimately by reading the Bible. Through his word we can understand his heart and his desires. Praying the words and desires of God ensures our petitions are aligned with his will.

In 2 Timothy 3:16-17 we learn that, "All Scripture *is* given by inspiration of God, and *is* profitable for doctrine, for reproof, for correction, for instruction in righteousness, that the man of God may be complete, thoroughly equipped for every good work."

Thus, praying scripture is a powerful practice that will make us everything God intended us to be and, therefore, equip us for every good work. Many scriptures contain commandments of the Lord. These commandments are what he wills for our lives, "...the things which I write to you are the commandments of the Lord."(1 Corinthians 14:37)

Praying in accordance to God's will is a part of the model prayer. Jesus instructed his disciples to pray in this manner: "Your kingdom come. *Your will* be done on earth as *it is* in heaven." (Matthew 6:10) Also, in Matthew 26:39 we are able to listen in on Jesus' prayer to God. Here he asks for God's will to be done even during his most difficult hours: "He went a little farther and fell on His face, and prayed, saying, 'O My Father, if it is possible, let this cup pass from me; nevertheless, *not as I will*, but as *you will*.'" (Matthew 26:39)

The opposite of praying God's will would be to pray for things that satisfy our selfish desires and have nothing to do with our sanctification and the glory of God. God does not answer these prayers. "You ask and do not receive, because you ask amiss, that you may spend *it* on your pleasures." (James 4:3)

We should habitually read the word of God for guidance, so we can pray in consonance with God's heart and desires.

We Must Pray with the Spirit and Understanding

"What is the conclusion then? I will pray with the spirit, and I will also pray with the understanding. I will sing with the spirit, and I will also sing with the understanding." (1 Corinthians 14:15)

PRAY WITH THE SPIRIT

Praying in the spirit comes when we are living out the Fruit of the Spirit and the Holy Spirit is actively working in our lives, interceding for us in prayer. "He (the Holy Spirit) makes intercession for the saints according to the will of God." (Romans 8:27)

PRAY WITH UNDERSTANDING

You can practice praying with understanding and wisdom in this manner:

Before you and your spouse pray, test the motives behind your petitions. Are your requests based on selfish desires or the desire to bring glory to God? Use the bible to examine the spirit behind your requests. Keep a journal for your prayer time. Use it to jot down your scripture vetted petitions. If there are any promises of God that authenticate your request, write these promises down and pray these words to him with faith and perseverance.

Also, have an open discussion with your spouse to make certain that you both are sincere about each request. This step is crucial in 'agreeing' or coming to the Lord in one accord as a couple. Conclude by praying audibly and distinctly so that you and your spouse can understand and join in on the prayer with a united spirit.

The opposite of praying with your spirit and with your understanding would be to use meaningless repetitions. "And when you pray, do not use vain repetitions as the heathen *do*. For they think that they will be heard for their many words." (Matthew 6:7)

Even if our words are coherent, if we repeat them just for the sake of praying 'something', we will fall into the routine of articulating vain words without feeling or meaning. We can certainly repeat our requests before God. However, we should pray these words with understanding and wisdom every time.

We Must Pray with Boldness and Sincerity

"Let us therefore come boldly to the throne of grace, that we may obtain mercy and find grace to help in time of need." (Hebrews 4:16)

Hannah came boldly before the throne of God as she poured out her soul in prayer. She was afflicted because of her empty womb, "She *was* in bitterness of soul, and prayed to the Lord and wept in anguish." She desired a child more than anything. She had a loving husband but was experiencing a bitter void because she wanted a child to mother. Her prayer to God was sincere and heartfelt. She came to God with a bold vow because she knew he could answer her prayer, "O Lord of hosts, if you will indeed look on the affliction of your maidservant and remember me, and not forget your maidservant, but will give your maidservant a male child, then I will give him to the Lord all the days of his life, and no razor shall come upon his head." (1 Samuel 1:11)

Then, "Eli said to her, "How long will you be drunk? Put your wine away from you!" But Hannah answered and said, "No, my lord, I *am* a woman of sorrowful spirit. I have drunk neither wine nor intoxicating drink, but have poured out my soul before the Lord." (1 Samuel 1:14-15)

Hannah was earnest in her request. She vowed to give her child to God all the days of his life. She prayed with boldness and sincerity and the Lord heard her prayer and responded. Her son, Samuel, became a prophet of the Lord. He was used powerfully to communicate God's messages to his people and their kings.

Here again we see an example of God answering a prayer, "...abundantly above all that we ask or think..." (Ephesians 3:20) Hannah did not ask for the authority and wisdom God gave to Samuel. She simply prayed earnestly and boldly knowing that God had the power to answer her prayer. God responded and blessed and used Samuel above all that Hannah could think or ask.

Likewise, when you and your spouse, come together in prayer you will find yourselves astonished and amazed at the power of God manifested. You too will experience that

God's answer to your prayers is, "...abundantly above all that you ask or think"

However, seeking and asking with all your heart is required. "Then you will call upon me and go and pray to me, and I will listen to you. And you will seek me and find *me*, when you search for me with all your heart." (Jeremiah 29:12-13) Praying with 'all your heart' means praying sincerely, genuinely and boldly. It is coming before God with the knowledge that he is *all*-powerful and that he is the only one that can make the seemingly impossible, possible.

The opposite of a sincere prayer is a prayer plagued with vanity and superficiality. We see such an example in the scribes, "And when you pray, you shall not be like the hypocrites. For they love to pray standing in the synagogues and on the corners of the streets, that they may be seen by men. Assuredly, I say to you, they have their reward." (Matthew 6:5) Impressing and pleasing people are egotistic and miserly motives. God knows our hearts and he can decipher whether our motives are sincere when others cannot. Prayer cannot be a ceremony or a ritual. Our words must be genuine. We must seek God earnestly and fervently.

Jesus said in one of his teachings, "Beware of the scribes, who desire to go around in long robes, love greetings in the marketplaces, the best seats in the synagogues, and the best places at feasts, who devour widows' houses, and for a pretense make long prayers. These will receive greater condemnation." (Mark 12:40)

He said that the scribes for a pretense made long prayers. In other words, they simulated long conversations with God, when in fact they were not communicating with God at all because they lacked sincerity. Their prayers were for show and were vain and empty.

David understood how important a sincere heart is for God. "Hear a just cause, O Lord, attend to my cry; Give ear to my prayer *which is* not from deceitful lips." (Psalm 17:1) He also encourages us to call upon God in truth, "The Lord *is* near to all who call upon Him, To all who call upon Him in truth." (Psalm 145:18)

Therefore, talk with your spouse before praying to discuss the sincerity of your requests. Are your petitions coming from an earnest heart? Surely, you have reasons why you want your supplications answered. Are these reasons in conformity with God's heart? Is the foundation for your prayers the glory of God? Or are you praying for things that satisfy self-serving desires? If this is so, ask God to give you a sincere heart. Ask his spirit to guide you to seek his will and his divine purposes in prayer.

We Must Pray in Faith

"But let him ask in faith, with no doubting, for he who doubts is like a wave of the sea driven and tossed by the wind. For let not that man suppose that he will receive anything from the Lord; he is a double-minded man, unstable in all his ways."(James 1:6-8)

The focus or object of our faith should be God; not our faith. When we do not pray in faith, we are believing one of two things: either God doesn't have the power to answer our prayers or God will not answer our prayers. If we believe he doesn't have the power, we are questioning his sovereignty and omnipotence. If we say he will not, we are questioning his faithfulness and kindness. To pray in faith means to believe God is willing and able because nothing is impossible for him.

Often times we pray and immediately we begin to use our logic to explain why God can't answer our prayer. We must pray in faith to experience a response from God. "Therefore I say to you, whatever things you ask when you pray, believe that you receive *them,* and you will have *them.*" *(*Mark 11:24)

Faith is believing that God will give us what he has promised. Also, when our faith is deeply rooted we accept God's response no matter if it is not what we expected or desired. Faith is believing God knows best and believing that in the end, no matter the circumstance, he will do us good for his glory. "…that He might humble you and that he might test you, to do you good in the end." (Deuteronomy 8:16)

We Must Pray with Humility

Couples who are humble do not care for public admiration. They do not seek fame nor recognition. They do not care for prestige. They do not exalt themselves before others nor do they exalt themselves before their own eyes. Unpretentiousness and reserve are two of their most notable characteristics.

In humility there is no self-praise or pride. Rather, the humble praise and give preference to others, "in honor giving preference to one another." (Romans 12:10) The humble do not seek the most prominent seats. They willingly take the lowest spot and prefer to go unnoticed and unnamed. The prayer of the humble is:

"Father do not let my vanity and pride reign, make me humble, meek and anonymous, so that it is your glory others may see."

Those who are humble do not focus on themselves. They focus on God and others. "With all lowliness and gentleness, with long-suffering, bearing with one another in love." (Ephesians 4:2)

The parable of the Pharisee and publican is a lesson on humility and pride. The Pharisee, was engulfed in self-regard, completely enveloped in self-centeredness, his security was erroneously founded on his deeds. He disdained the publican who was praying earnestly pouring his heart out before God.

The publican understood he was a sinner. He was submerged in the acknowledgement of his lowliness. So much so that he did not lift his eyes toward heaven but with humble expression beat his breast and pleaded, "God be merciful to me, a sinner!"

Jesus gives us the result of each of these men's approaches to prayer. One was as far from humility as the east is from the west. The other was overtaken with lowliness of spirit and humbleness of heart.

"If my people who are called by my name will humble themselves, and pray and seek my face, and turn from their wicked ways, then I will hear from heaven, and will forgive their sin and heal their land." (2 Chronicles 7:14)

Did God hear the publican and forgive his sin? Following is the full account of this parable as told by Jesus.

"Also He spoke this parable to some who trusted in themselves that they were righteous, and despised others: "Two men went up to the temple to pray, one a Pharisee and the other a tax collector. The Pharisee stood and prayed thus with himself, 'God, I thank You that I am not like other men - extortioners, unjust, adulterers, or even as this tax collector. I fast twice a week; I give tithes of all that I possess.' And the tax collector, standing afar off, would not so much as raise *his* eyes to heaven, but beat his breast, saying, 'God, be merciful to me a sinner!' I tell you, this man went down to his house justified *rather* than the other; for everyone who exalts himself will be humbled, and he who humbles himself will be exalted." (Luke 18:9-14)

The self-righteous and smug Pharisee congratulated and exalted himself in prayer. He relied on his deeds instead of relying on God. Such a person will not be accepted by God because, "God resists the proud, but gives grace to the humble." (James 4:6)

So, come before God with your spouse putting your merits aside and resting solely on God's grace in humbleness. He will give you grace and freely justify you.

Chapter 5

PERSISTENCE IN PRAYER

We Must Be Persistent In Our Prayers

It is essential that spouses persist in prayer. There are two parables that we will look at in detail, in which Jesus teaches that we should always pray and not faint. When you and your spouse give up and cease to pray you are communicating one of three things:

1. You believe God will not answer.

2. You have become neglectful in your responsibility to pray.

3. Your request has lost importance to you.

Jesus communicates through two parables that it is important we pray persistently. Persistently means to continue firmly or unwaveringly in a course of action in spite of difficulty or opposition. It means to endure in your desire to be answered, even if your circumstances do not presently align with the response you seek. Jesus crowns the parable of the friend who at midnight begged persistently for three loaves of bread, with these words, "Ask, and it will be given to you; seek, and you will find; knock, and it will be opened to you." (Luke 11:9).

When we knock because we know a dear friend is inside who can help with a situation of great importance, we do not waver or knock weakly. We firmly clinch our fist and give the door a good firm, solid knock. If we do not get a response, we do not walk away. We persist and knock firmly, again. We wait and knock firmly, wait and knock firmly and we repeat this cycle persistently until the door is opened and our friend answers.

The same applies to God. We pray because we know he is there. He is dear to us and we are dear to him. He gave his only son, which is the highest price he could pay. Will he not give us everything else we need? "He who did not spare His own Son, but delivered Him up for us all, how shall He not with Him also freely give us all things?" (Romans 8:32)

So, knock firmly, knock persistently and he will answer. Do not give in and do not faint. Let's look at this parable Jesus told found in Luke 11:5-9.

PARABLE #1 A PERSISTENT FRIEND IN NEED

"Which of you shall have a friend, and go to him at midnight and say to him, 'Friend, lend me three loaves; for a friend of mine has come to me on his journey, and I have nothing to set before him'; and he will answer from within and say, 'Do not trouble me; the door is now shut, and my children are with me in bed; I cannot rise and give to you' I say to you, though he will not rise and give to him because he is his friend, yet because of his persistence he will rise and give him as many as he needs. So I say to you, ask, and it will be given to you; seek, and you will find; knock, and it will be opened to you." (Luke 11:5-9).

In this parable the primary reason the petitioner was answered was not because of his 'friend' status. Notice the words of Jesus, "though he will not rise and give to him because he is his *friend*, yet because of his persistence he will rise and give him as many as he needs." Here we learn that the petitioner was answered because of his persistence. The circumstance did not seem to align with the response this petitioner required. The door was already shut, the children were in bed, the owner of the loaves of bread was also in bed and he said, "I cannot rise and give to you."

Now, let's think of our God. Our God doesn't sleep. He doesn't need rest. There is no such thing as an inopportune time to call on him. He is available twenty four-seven. He is all powerful and has more riches than our finite mind can understand. Everything and everyone is subject to his omnipotence. This strong and mighty God has called us to persist in prayer and he has also called us his friends, "You are my friends if you do whatever I command you. No longer do I call you servants, for a servant does not know what his master is doing; but I have called you friends, for all things that I heard from my Father I have made known to you." (John 15:14-15)

He, this incomparable God, is inviting your and your spouse to persist in prayer. So, do. Persevere! Continue to ask, seek and knock. When the time is right God will respond.

Barnes says in his commentary on this parable:

"This is to be applied to God in no other sense than that he often hears prayers and grants blessings even long after they appear to be unanswered or withheld. He leaves them to persevere for months or years, until they feel entirely their dependence on him, until they see that they can obtain the blessing in no other way, and until they are prepared to receive it. Often they are not prepared to receive it when they ask it at first. They may be proud, or have no just sense of their dependence, or they would not value the blessing, or it may at that time not be best for them to obtain it. But let no one despair. If the thing is for our good, and if it is proper that it should be granted, God will give it. Let us first ask aright; let us see that our minds are in a proper state; let us feel our need of the blessing; let us inquire whether God has promised such a blessing, and then let us persevere until God gives it." (Barnes Commentary of Luke)

It is certain that we are limited in our view of the world and the spiritual battles going on around us. We cannot see the future or know the circumstances that influence situations beyond our realm of knowledge. God, however, sees and knows everything. He will respond at the most opportune time. His response comes when we are ready to give him the glory and it will come in a way that is aligned with His sovereign will.

You and your spouse can confidently rest and rejoice in the fact that he gives "…abundantly above all that we ask or think." (Ephesians 3:20) when we persist in prayer.

PARABLE #2 THE WIDOW WANTING JUSTICE

There is also another parable in which Jesus teaches that we should always pray and not faint. This is the parable of the unjust steward.

He spoke a parable to them, that men should always pray and not lose heart, saying: "There was in a certain city a judge who did not fear God nor regard man. Now there was a widow in that city; and she came to him, saying, 'Get justice for me from my adversary.' And he would not for a while; but afterward he said within himself, 'Though I do not fear God nor regard man, yet because this widow troubles me I will avenge her, lest by her continual coming she weary me.'" Then the Lord said, "Hear what the unjust judge said. And shall God not avenge His own elect who cry out day and night to Him, though He bears long with them? I tell you that He will avenge them speedily." (Luke 18:1-8)

In this parable the judge did not fear God nor regard or value man. He simply responded to the widow because she troubled or disturbed him. He didn't want to be bothered by her continual presence requesting justice from her adversary. Therefore, he responded and avenged her. Jesus reiterates, "Hear what the unjust judge said. And shall God not avenge His own elect who cry out day and night to Him, though He bears long with them? I tell you that He will avenge them speedily." (Luke 18: 6-8)

We are his elect. Jesus said, "You did not choose Me, but *I chose you* and appointed you that you should go and bear fruit, and that your fruit should remain, that whatever you ask the Father in my name he may give you." (John 15:16) What a gift! Being his fruit bearing elect and having prayers answered is one in the same. Because we are his elect we should bear fruit. Have you wondered why he gives us what we ask for when we bear fruit? The reason is: we bear fruit when we are attached to the vine that is Jesus. When we are attached, meaning we have an intimate relationship with him, we have his mind and understand his purposes. Our goals and desires are his goals and desires. Therefore, we pray in alignment to his will and for his glory. Without him we can do nothing. This includes praying for the right purposes. "I am the vine, you *are* the branches. He who abides in Me, and I in him, bears much fruit; for *without Me you can do nothing*." (John 15:5)

Praying *persistently* and *in line with God's purpose* is a powerful formula for receiving a response from God. Praying persistently is an expression of great faith. Through consistency in prayer we communicate that we depend solely on him, believe in him and accept his perfect time.

When the Syro-Phoenician woman came to Jesus, he seemed to disregard her pleas. However, she would not be turned away. Jesus listened to every comment that came from her indecorous importunity, and said, " 'O woman, great *is* your faith! Let it be to you as you desire.' And her daughter was healed from that very hour." (Matt. 15:28)

When a determined husband and wife set out to achieve something, if they do not achieve it the first, second or twentieth time, they continue to insist until they do achieve it. Likewise a committed husband and wife of prayer, when they begin to pray for something of importance, they continue to pray for it until they obtain what they are after. We should always pray in accordance to God's will and when we do begin to pray we should never give up praying until we get a response from God, or until God reveals that it is not his will to grant us what we have requested.

Without a doubt there will be times when God will respond the first time we ask; but there will be many times when we must pray repeatedly and persistently before God will answer.

Our Continual Responsibility to Pray

When we study the Greek word *proskartereo* we can more clearly understand the importance of constant prayer. *Proskartereo* begins with 'pros', which means, 'toward, in the direction of' and 'kartereo' which means, 'to be strong, firm'. When we put these two definitions together we see that the word means, "to be strong toward something or someone." As it is used in the New Testament the word means, 'to be steadfastly attentive unto, to give unremitting care to something, to persevere and not to faint, to show one's courage for, to be in constant readiness, to wait on constantly.'

Five of the ten occurrences of this word in the Greek New Testament are used in admonition to pray. No other act is stressed with this accent. Not going to church, being hospitable, preaching, utilizing a gift or offering. Each of the five incidents in which the word is used are in a continuous action tense. This gives special importance to the sustained responsibility we have to pray.

The following scriptures contain the ten occurrences of this word in the New Testament.

Mark 3:9 - of the time when Jesus told His disciples to keep a small boat ready for Him because of the multitude

Acts 1:14 - of the disciples detailing they all continued with one accord in prayer

Acts 2:42,46 - of the converts' faithful following of the doctrine, instruction, fellowship, breaking of bread and prayer

Acts 6:4 - of the apostles commitment to prayer and teaching of the word

Acts 8:13 - of Simon's close following of Philip

Acts 10:7 - of the soldiers who stood ready to met every wish or command of Cornelius

Romans 12:12 - an admonition from Paul to the Roman Christians to persevere in prayer

Romans 13:6 - of government officials' focus on their duties

Colossians 4:2 - other admonition from Paul for believers to give specific attention to prayer.

Again, note that *five* of these scriptures have to do with persistent prayer.

It has been said that, "prayer is the most important thing we do as believers, and the easiest thing to neglect." Every person God used powerfully in the Bible was a person of prayer. Likewise, anyone who today experiences God's works in a mighty way and is used powerfully by him, cultivates an intimate relationship with him through prayer. As an example, Peter and Paul were men of prayer, who left us important guidance about the power of prayer and its relation to knowing God intimately.

The ultimate example is Jesus, who though He was perfect, sinless, and always obedient to the Father's will, saw the importance of constant communion with God in prayer. He set the standard for prayer. If Jesus needed to pray, how much more do you and I? As we read the gospels we can note everything that Jesus did and said with regard to prayer. The gospels record that in the last twenty-four hours of Jesus' life he prayed at least eleven times.

Chapter 6

PRAYING SCRIPTURE

Praying Scripture Expresses Faith In God's Word

When you and your spouse pray scripture, you acknowledge the authority of God's Word and express faith that each of God's promises are true. Praying through scripture with a humble heart will begin removing obstacles such as we have discussed in previous chapters: fear, erroneous motives, sin in our lives or a lack of faith. As we read the word of God and delight in a conversation with him about his reveled will and promises, we grow in our relationship with him.

Remember that even though there are innumerable benefits to praying in alignment with scripture, the specific words you utter are not as important as the heart with which they are spoken. John Bunyan said, "It is better for our heart to be without words than our words to be without heart. What a comfort to know that in those times when we are in such distress or grief that we cannot even frame words to express our need, the Holy Spirit is interceding on our behalf in accordance with God's will."

When we cannot pray as we should, "… the Spirit also helps in our weaknesses. For we do not know what we should pray for as we ought, but the Spirit Himself makes intercession for us with groanings which cannot be uttered." (Romans 8:26)

How To Pray Scripture

Studying the Bible and speaking to God through prayer are the chief methods for developing an intimate relationship with him. All other spiritual behaviors or disciplines such as: worship, fasting, service and ministry, part from the premises of growing from his word and praying. Prayer and scripture reading can be seen as individual spiritual practices. However, they can be even more compelling and powerful when they are integrated into one discipline of "praying scripture."

Are you ever at a loss about what you should pray for? Do your prayers ever become dull and repetitious? Your boldness and confidence in prayer will be renewed when you pray God's words. How exactly do we pray scripture? To pray scripture is to formulate your prayers modeling after a particular passage or passages in the Bible. You may do this by praying through topical scriptures, praying God's promises or using prayers in the bible as guides to communicate with God.

PRAYERS OF THE BIBLE

The prayers of the Bible, especially the Lord's Prayer (Luke 11:1-4, Matthew 6:9-13) become supports that teach us how to communicate with God.

The Lord's Prayer gives us the components that should comprise our prayers. "Our Father in heaven" teaches us that we are praying to our father. A father that cares about us and is ready to listen to our pleas. "Hallowed be your name" expresses our desire to bring glory to God with our every word and action. The phrase "your kingdom come, your will be done on earth as it is in heaven" is a reminder that we are to desire and seek God's will for our lives and the world around us. We are also taught to ask for what we need, "give this day our daily bread." "Forgive us our debts, as we forgive our debtors" reminds us to forgive others as God has forgiven us. The end of the Lord's Prayer, "And lead us not into temptation, but deliver us from evil" is a call for help in attaining victory over sin and a plea for safekeeping from the attacks of the devil.

The Lord's Prayer is one prayer in the bible. Aside from this prayer there are many more. The entire book of Psalms is composed of prayers. We may use these prayers in the bible as guides when talking to God.

PRAYING PARTS OF SCRIPTURE

As we read the stories, history, poems, prose and parables of God's word and we pay attention to the spirit or application behind each text, we can identify with the message as it applies to our daily lives and the world around us. These scripture-inspired thoughts, as we engage with God in conversation, turn into pleas, worship, confession, thanksgiving, and praise for God's revealed will for our lives. Our devotionals, as we read scripture and speak with God, become an integration of reading and prayer.

PRAYING PASSAGES ON A PARTICULAR TOPIC

You may also search for topical passages in the Bible that reflect your present need, your yearning for worship, your desire to give thanks, the need for confession or encouragement, your passion for the expansion of his kingdom or your desire to bring glory to his name. If you are praying for a loved one, pray through and claim promises that God has given us about intercession for others. The following chapters of this book contain topical scriptures and biblical promises that you may use to pray with your spouse.

STEPS FOR PRAYING SCRIPTURE

1. Ask God to reveal the truth of his word to you through the Holy Spirit.

2. Select a passage and pay attention to the spirit or message of the text. Identify with the message as it applies to you.

3. Read carefully through your passage(s) as you meditate on each word.

4. As you meditate on the message of the passage bring this message into your conversation with God. Remember

that the specific words we utter are not as important as the heart with which they are communicated.

5. Make time to pray to God in alignment with his word on a daily basis.

Chapter 7

TOPICAL SCRIPTURES

FOR PRAYING

WITH YOUR SPOUSE

Praying for Restoration of Our Love
Toward God and Others

GOD'S LOVE FOR US

For God so loved the world that he gave his only begotten son, that whoever believes in him should not perish but have everlasting life. John 3:16

But God demonstrates his own love toward us, in that while we were still sinners, Christ died for us. Romans 5:8

Who shall separate us from the love of Christ? *Shall* tribulation, or distress, or persecution, or famine, or nakedness, or peril, or sword? As it is written:

"For Your sake we are killed all day long; we are accounted as sheep for the slaughter." Yet in all these things we are more than conquerors through Him who loved us. For I am persuaded that neither death nor life, nor angels nor principalities nor powers, nor things present nor things to come, nor height nor depth, nor any other created thing, shall be able to separate us from the love of God which is in Christ Jesus our Lord.
Romans 8:35–39

In this is love, not that we loved God, but that He loved us and sent His Son *to be* the propitiation for our sins.
1 John 4:10

OUR RECIPROCAL LOVE TOWARD HIM

If you love me, keep my commandments. John 14:15

He who has my commandments and keeps them, it is he who loves me. And he who loves me will be loved by my Father, and I will love him and manifest myself to him. Judas (not Iscariot) said to Him, "Lord, how is it that you will manifest Yourself to us, and not to the world?" Jesus answered and said to him, "If anyone loves me, he will keep my word; and my Father will love him, and we will come to him and make our home with him. He who does not love me does not keep my words; and the word which you hear is not mine but the Father's who sent me. John 14:21–24

For the love of Christ compels us, because we judge thus: that if one died for all, then all died; and He died for all, that those who live should live no longer for themselves, but for Him who died for them and rose again.
2 Corinthians 5:14–15

LOVING ONE ANOTHER

And the second, like *it, is* this: 'You shall love your neighbor as yourself.' There is no other commandment greater than these. Mark 12:31

A new commandment I give to you, that you love one another; as I have loved you, that you also love one another. By this all will know that you are my disciples, if you have love for one another. John 13:34–35

As the Father loved me, I also have loved you; abide in my love. If you keep my commandments, you will abide in my love, just as I have kept My Father's commandments and abide in His love. These things I have spoken to you, that my joy may remain in you, and *that* your joy may be full. This is my commandment, that you love one another as I have loved you. Greater love has no one than this, than to lay down one's life for his friends. You are my friends if you do whatever I command you. No longer do I call you servants, for a servant does not know what his master is doing; but I have called you friends, for all things that I heard from my Father I have made known to you. You did not choose me, but I chose you and appointed you that you should go and bear fruit, and *that* your fruit should remain, that whatever you ask the Father in my name he may give you. These things I command you, that you love one another. John 15:9–17

Let love *be* without hypocrisy. Abhor what is evil. Cling to what is good. *Be* kindly affectionate to one another with brotherly love, in honor giving preference to one another. Romans 12:9–10

Owe no one anything except to love one another, for he who loves another has fulfilled the law. For the commandments, "You shall not commit adultery," "You shall not murder," "You shall not steal," "You shall not bear false witness," "You shall not covet," and if *there is* any other commandment, are *all* summed up in this saying, namely, "You shall love your neighbor as yourself." Love does no harm to a neighbor; therefore love *is* the fulfillment of the law. Romans 13:8–10

Therefore, as *the* elect of God, holy and beloved, put on tender mercies, kindness, humility, meekness, longsuffering; bearing with one another, and forgiving one another, if anyone has a complaint against another; even as Christ forgave you, so you also *must do*. But above all these things put on love, which is the bond of perfection. Colossians 3:12–14

Now the purpose of the commandment is love from a pure heart, *from* a good conscience, and *from* sincere faith. 1 Timothy 1:5

Since you have purified your souls in obeying the truth through the Spirit in sincere love of the brethren, love one another fervently with a pure heart. 1 Peter 1:22

Beloved, let us love one another, for love is of God; and everyone who loves is born of God and knows God. He who does not love does not know God, for God is love. In this the love of God was manifested toward us, that God has sent His only begotten Son into the world, that we might live through Him. In this is love, not that we loved God, but that He loved us and sent His Son *to be* the propitiation for our sins. Beloved, if God so loved us, we also ought to love one another. 1 John 4:7–12

LOVING OUR ENEMIES

You have heard that it was said, 'You shall love your neighbor and hate your enemy.' But I say to you, love your enemies, bless those who curse you, do good to those who hate you, and pray for those who spitefully use you and persecute you, that you may be sons of your Father in heaven; for He makes His sun rise on the evil and on the good, and sends rain on the just and on the unjust.
Matthew 5:43–45

But I say to you who hear: Love your enemies, do good to those who hate you, bless those who curse you, and pray for those who spitefully use you. To him who strikes you on the *one* cheek, offer the other also. And from him, who takes away your cloak, do not withhold *your* tunic either. Give to everyone who asks of you. And from him who takes away your goods do not ask *them* back. And just as you want men to do to you, you also do to them likewise.
Luke 6:27–32

TRUE LOVE

Though I speak with the tongues of men and of angels, but have not love, I have become sounding brass or a clanging cymbal. And though I have *the gift of* prophecy, and understand all mysteries and all knowledge, and though I have all faith, so that I could remove mountains, but have not love, I am nothing. And though I bestow all my goods to feed *the poor,* and though I give my body to be burned, but have not love, it profits me nothing.

Love suffers long *and* is kind; love does not envy; love does not parade itself, is not puffed up; does not behave rudely, does not seek its own, is not provoked, thinks no evil; does not rejoice in iniquity, but rejoices in the truth; bears all things, believes all things, hopes all things, endures all things.

Love never fails. But whether *there are* prophecies, they will fail; whether *there are* tongues, they will cease; whether *there is* knowledge, it will vanish away. For we know in part and we prophesy in part. But when that which is perfect has come, then that which is in part will be done away.

When I was a child, I spoke as a child, I understood as a child, I thought as a child; but when I became a man, I put away childish things. For now we see in a mirror, dimly, but then face to face. Now I know in part, but then I shall know just as I also am known.

And now abide faith, hope, love, these three; but the greatest of these *is* love. 1 Corinthians 13:1–13

Praying for Victory In Spiritual Battles

FOR CAPTIVATING EVERY THOUGHT

For though we walk in the flesh, we do not war according to the flesh. For the weapons of our warfare *are* not carnal but mighty in God for pulling down strongholds, casting down arguments and every high thing that exalts itself against the knowledge of God, bringing every thought into captivity to the obedience of Christ.
2 Corinthians 10:3–5

Bearing with one another, and forgiving one another, if anyone has a complaint against another; even as Christ forgave you, so you also *must do*. But above all these things put on love, which is the bond of perfection. And let the peace of God rule in your hearts, to which also you were called in one body; and be thankful. Colossians 3:13-15

Inasmuch then as the children have partaken of flesh and blood, He Himself likewise shared in the same, that through death He might destroy him who had the power of death, that is, the devil. Hebrews 2:14

The devil, who deceived them, was cast into the lake of fire and brimstone where the beast and the false prophet *are*. And they will be tormented day and night forever and ever. Revelation 20:10

FOR SELF-CONTROL AND VIGILANCE

Be sober; be vigilant; because your adversary the devil walks about like a roaring lion, seeking whom he may devour. Resist him, steadfast in the faith, knowing that the same sufferings are experienced by your brotherhood in the world. 1 Peter 5:8–9

FOR NOT GIVING THE DEVIL A FOOTHOLD

"Be angry, and do not sin" Do not let the sun go down on your wrath, nor give place to the devil.
Ephesians 4:26–27

MAINTAINING SUSTAINED INTIMACY WITHIN MARRIAGE

Do not deprive one another except with consent for a time that you may give yourselves to fasting and prayer; and come together again so that Satan does not tempt you because of your lack of self-control. 1 Corinthians 7:5

FOR THE ABILITY TO FORGIVE

Now whom you forgive anything, I also *forgive*. For if indeed I have forgiven anything, I have forgiven that one for your sakes in the presence of Christ, lest Satan should take advantage of us; for we are not ignorant of his devices.
2 Corinthians 2:10–11

And no wonder! For Satan himself transforms himself into an angel of light. Therefore it is no great thing if his ministers also transform themselves into ministers of righteousness, whose end will be according to their works.
2 Corinthians 11:14–15

SATAN UNDER OUR FEET

And the God of peace will crush Satan under your feet shortly. The grace of our Lord Jesus Christ *be* with you. Amen. Romans 16:20

FOR BEING KIND AND NOT QUARRELING

And a servant of the Lord must not quarrel but be gentle to all, able to teach, patient, in humility correcting those who are in opposition, if God perhaps will grant them repentance, so that they may know the truth, and *that* they may come to their senses *and escape* the snare of the devil, having been taken captive by him to *do* his will.
2 Timothy 2:24–26

FOR UNMASKING ENVY AND AMBITION

But if you have bitter envy and self-seeking in your hearts, do not boast and lie against the truth. This wisdom does not descend from above, but *is* earthly, sensual, and demonic. James 3:14–15

DO RIGHT, BE RIGHTEOUS, AS GOD IS RIGHTEOUS

Little children, let no one deceive you. He who practices righteousness is righteous, just as He is righteous. He who sins is of the devil, for the devil has sinned from the beginning. For this purpose the Son of God was manifested, that He might destroy the works of the devil. Whoever has been born of God does not sin, for His seed remains in him; and he cannot sin, because he has been born of God. In this the children of God and the children of the devil are manifest: Whoever does not practice righteousness is not of God, nor *is* he who does not love his brother. 1 John 3:7–10

RESISTING SATAN

Therefore submit to God. Resist the devil and he will flee from you. James 4:7

STANDING FIRM USING GOD'S FULL ARMOR

Finally, my brethren, be strong in the Lord and in the power of His might. Put on the whole armor of God, that you may be able to stand against the wiles of the devil. For we do not wrestle against flesh and blood, but against principalities, against powers, against the rulers of the darkness of this age, against spiritual *hosts* of wickedness in the heavenly *places*. Therefore take up the whole armor of God, that you may be able to withstand in the evil day, and having done all, to stand.

Stand therefore, having girded your waist with truth, having put on the breastplate of righteousness, and having shod your feet with the preparation of the gospel of peace; above all, taking the shield of faith with which you will be able to quench all the fiery darts of the wicked one. And take the helmet of salvation, and the sword of the Spirit, which is the word of God. Ephesians 6:10–17

FOR OTHERS IN SPIRITUAL BATTLE

Praying always with all prayer and supplication in the Spirit, being watchful to this end with all perseverance and supplication for all the saints - and for me, that utterance may be given to me, that I may open my mouth boldly to make known the mystery of the gospel, for which I am an ambassador in chains; that in it I may speak boldly, as I ought to speak. Ephesians 6:18–20

Finally, brethren, pray for us, that the word of the Lord may run *swiftly* and be glorified, just as *it is* with you, and that we may be delivered from unreasonable and wicked men; for not all have faith. But the Lord is faithful, who will establish you and guard *you* from the evil one.
2 Thessalonians 3:1–3

Praying For Unity

UNITING IN PRAYER

Again I say to you that if two of you agree on earth concerning anything that they ask, it will be done for them by my Father in heaven. For where two or three are gathered together in my name, I am there in the midst of them. Matthew 18:19-20

THE UNITY JESUS DESIRES

Now I am no longer in the world, but these are in the world, and I come to you. Holy Father, keep through your name those whom you have given me, that they may be one as we *are*. "I do not pray for these alone, but also for those who will believe in me through their word; that they all may be one, as you, Father, *are* in me, and I in you; that they also may be one in us, that the world may believe that you sent me. And the glory which you gave me I have given them, that they may be one just as we are one: I in them, and you in me; that they may be made perfect in one, and that the world may know that you have sent me, and have loved them as you have loved me." John 17:11, 20-23

UNITY THAT GLORIFIES GOD

Now may the God of patience and comfort grant you to be like-minded toward one another, according to Christ Jesus, that you may with one mind *and* one mouth glorify the God and Father of our Lord Jesus Christ. Therefore receive one another, just as Christ also received us, to the glory of God. Romans 15:5-7

THE UNITY OF THE BODY OF CHRIST

For I say, through the grace given to me, to everyone who is among you, not to think *of himself* more highly than he ought to think, but to think soberly, as God has dealt to each one a measure of faith. For as we have many members in one body, but all the members do not have the same function, so we, *being* many, are one body in Christ, and individually members of one another. Having then gifts differing according to the grace that is given to us, *let us use them:* if prophecy, *let us prophesy* in proportion to our faith; or ministry, *let us use it* in *our* ministering; he who teaches, in teaching; he who exhorts, in exhortation; he who gives, with liberality; he who leads, with diligence; he who shows mercy, with cheerfulness. Romans 12:3-8

For as the body is one and has many members, but all the members of that one body, being many, are one body, so also *is* Christ. For by one Spirit we were all baptized into one body—whether Jews or Greeks, whether slaves or free—and have all been made to drink into one Spirit. 1 Corinthians 12:12-13

But our presentable *parts* have no need. But God composed the body, having given greater honor to that *part* which lacks it, that there should be no schism in the body, but *that* the members should have the same care for one another. And if one member suffers, all the members suffer with *it;* or if one member is honored, all the members rejoice with *it*. Now you are the body of Christ, and members individually. 1 Corinthians 12:24-27

Therefore, putting away lying, "*Let* each one *of you* speak truth with his neighbor," for we are members of one another. Ephesians 4:25

And let the peace of God rule in your hearts, to which also you were called in one body; and be thankful. Let the word of Christ dwell in you richly in all wisdom, teaching and admonishing one another in psalms and hymns and spiritual songs, singing with grace in your hearts to the Lord. And whatever you do in word or deed, *do* all in the name of the Lord Jesus, giving thanks to God the Father through Him. Colossians 3:15-17

ONE IN HEART & MIND- ONE BODY & SPIRIT

Now the multitude of those who believed were of one heart and one soul; neither did anyone say that any of the things he possessed was his own, but they had all things in common. And with great power the apostles gave witness to the resurrection of the Lord Jesus. And great grace was upon them all. Acts 4:32-33

Now I plead with you, brethren, by the name of our Lord Jesus Christ, that you all speak the same thing, and *that* there be no divisions among you, but *that* you be perfectly joined together in the same mind and in the same judgment.
1 Corinthians 1:10

Finally, brethren, farewell. Become complete. Be of good comfort, be of one mind, live in peace; and the God of love and peace will be with you.
2 Corinthians 13:11

I, therefore, the prisoner of the Lord, beseech you to walk worthy of the calling with which you were called, with all lowliness and gentleness, with longsuffering, bearing with one another in love, endeavoring to keep the unity of the Spirit in the bond of peace. *There is* one body and one Spirit, just as you were called in one hope of your calling; one Lord, one faith, one baptism; one God and Father of all, who *is* above all, and through all, and in you all.
Ephesians 4:1-6

I implore Euodia and I implore Syntyche to be of the same mind in the Lord. Philippians 4:2

UNITED IN LOVE

Let love *be* without hypocrisy. Abhor what is evil. Cling to what is good. *Be* kindly affectionate to one another with brotherly love, in honor giving preference to one another; not lagging in diligence, fervent in spirit, serving the Lord;

rejoicing in hope, patient in tribulation, continuing steadfastly in prayer; distributing to the needs of the saints, given to hospitality. Bless those who persecute you; bless and do not curse. Rejoice with those who rejoice, and weep with those who weep. Be of the same mind toward one another. Do not set your mind on high things, but associate with the humble. Do not be wise in your own opinion.
Romans 12:9-16

Owe no one anything except to love one another, for he who loves another has fulfilled the law.
Romans 13:8

Therefore if *there is* any consolation in Christ, if any comfort of love, if any fellowship of the Spirit, if any affection and mercy, fulfill my joy by being like-minded, having the same love, *being* of one accord, of one mind.
Philippians 2:1-2

That their hearts may be encouraged, being knit together in love, and *attaining* to all riches of the full assurance of understanding, to the knowledge of the mystery of God, both of the Father and of Christ, in whom are hidden all the treasures of wisdom and knowledge. Colossians 2:2-3

Finally, all *of you be* of one mind, having compassion for one another; love as brothers, *be* tenderhearted, *be* courteous; not returning evil for evil or reviling for reviling, but on the contrary blessing, knowing that you were called to this, that you may inherit a blessing. 1 Peter 3:8-9

Praying for a Christian Conduct

FOR HOLINESS

I beseech you therefore, brethren, by the mercies of God, that you present your bodies a living sacrifice, holy, acceptable to God, *which is* your reasonable service. And do not be conformed to this world, but be transformed by the renewing of your mind, that you may prove what *is* that good and acceptable and perfect will of God. Rom. 12:1–2

Or do you not know that your body is the temple of the Holy Spirit *who is* in you, whom you have from God, and you are not your own? For you were bought at a price; therefore glorify God in your body and in your spirit, which are God's. I Corinthians 6:19–20

But fornication and all uncleanness or covetousness, let it not even be named among you, as is fitting for saints. Ephesians 5:3

And you, who once were alienated and enemies in your mind by wicked works, yet now He has reconciled in the body of His flesh through death, to present you holy, and blameless, and above reproach in His sight.
Colossians 1:21–22

Therefore, as *the* elect of God, holy and beloved, put on tender mercies, kindness, humility, meekness, long-suffering; bearing with one another, and forgiving one another, if anyone has a complaint against another; even as Christ forgave you, so you also *must do*.
Colossians 3:12–13

So that He may establish your hearts blameless in holiness before our God and Father at the coming of our Lord Jesus Christ with all His saints.
1 Thessalonians 3:13

For this is the will of God, your sanctification: that you should abstain from sexual immorality; that each of you should know how to possess his own vessel in sanctification and honor, not in passion of lust, like the Gentiles who do not know God; that no one should take advantage of and defraud his brother in this matter, because the Lord *is* the avenger of all such, as we also forewarned you and testified. For God did not call us to uncleanness, but in holiness. Therefore he who rejects *this* does not reject man, but God, who has also given us His Holy Spirit.
1 Thessalonians 4:3–8

Therefore do not be ashamed of the testimony of our Lord, nor of me His prisoner, but share with me in the sufferings for the gospel according to the power of God, who has saved us and called *us* with a holy calling, not according to our works, but according to His own purpose and grace which was given to us in Christ Jesus before time began. 2 Timothy 1:8–9

Pursue peace with all *people,* and holiness, without which no one will see the Lord. Hebrews 12:14

As obedient children, not conforming yourselves to the former lusts, *as* in your ignorance; but as He who called you *is* holy, you also be holy in all *your* conduct, because it is written, "Be holy, for I am holy." 1 Peter 1:14-16

But you *are* a chosen generation, a royal priesthood, a holy nation, His own special people, that you may proclaim the praises of Him who called you out of darkness into His marvelous light; who once *were* not a people but *are* now the people of God, who had not obtained mercy but now have obtained mercy. 1 Peter 2:9–10

Therefore, since all these things will be dissolved, what manner *of persons* ought you to be in holy conduct and godliness, looking for and hastening the coming of the day of God, because of which the heavens will be dissolved, being on fire, and the elements will melt with fervent heat? Nevertheless we, according to His promise, look for new heavens and a new earth in which righteousness dwells.
2 Peter 3:11–13

FOR SPIRITUAL EXAMINATION

Search me, O God, and know my heart;
Try me, and know my anxieties;
And see if *there is any* wicked way in me,
And lead me in the way everlasting.
Psalm 139:23–24

FOR THE CONFESSION OF SIN AND REPENTANCE

Blessed *is he whose* transgression *is* forgiven,
Whose sin *is* covered.
Blessed *is* the man to whom the Lord
does not impute iniquity,
And in whose spirit *there is* no deceit.
When I kept silent, my bones grew old
Through my groaning all the daylong.

For day and night your hand was heavy upon me;
My vitality was turned into the drought of summer.
I acknowledged my sin to you,
And my iniquity I have not hidden.
I said, "I will confess my transgressions
to the Lord,"
And you forgave the iniquity of my sin.
For this cause everyone who is godly
shall pray to you
In a time when you may be found;
Surely in a flood of great waters
They shall not come near him. Psalm 32:1–6

Have mercy upon me, O God,
According to Your loving kindness;
According to the multitude of Your tender mercies,
Blot out my transgressions.
Wash me thoroughly from my iniquity,
And cleanse me from my sin.
For I acknowledge my transgressions,
And my sin *is* always before me.
Against You, You only, have I sinned,
And done *this* evil in Your sight—
That You may be found just when You speak,
And blameless when You judge.
Behold, I was brought forth in iniquity,
And in sin my mother conceived me.
Behold, You desire truth in the inward parts,
And in the hidden *part*
You will make me to know wisdom.
Purge me with hyssop, and I shall be clean;
Wash me, and I shall be whiter than snow.
Make me hear joy and gladness,

That the bones you have broken may rejoice.
Hide your face from my sins,
And blot out all my iniquities.
Create in me a clean heart, O God,
And renew a steadfast spirit within me.
Do not cast me away from your presence,
And do not take Your Holy Spirit from me.
Restore to me the joy of your salvation,
And uphold me *by your* generous Spirit.
Then I will teach transgressors your ways,
And sinners shall be converted to you.
Deliver me from the guilt of bloodshed, O God,
The God of my salvation,
And my tongue shall
sing aloud of your righteousness.
O Lord, open my lips,
And my mouth shall show forth your praise.
For you do not desire sacrifice,
or else I would give *it;*
You do not delight in burnt offering.
The sacrifices of God *are* a broken spirit,
A broken and a contrite heart
These, O God, You will not despise. Psalm 51:1–17

Confess *your* trespasses to one another, and pray for one another, that you may be healed. The effective, fervent prayer of a righteous man avails much.
James 5:16

If we confess our sins, He is faithful and just to forgive us *our* sins and to cleanse us from all unrighteousness.
1 John 1:9

FOR THE WILLINGNESS TO FORGIVE

Take heed to yourselves. If your brother sins against you, rebuke him; and if he repents, forgive him. And if he sins against you seven times in a day, and seven times in a day returns to you, saying, 'I repent,' you shall forgive him. Luke 17:3–4

Praying for The Will of God

I delight to do your will, O my God, and your law *is* within my heart. Psalm 40:8

Behold, You desire truth in the inward parts, and in the hidden *part* You will make me to know wisdom. Psalm 51:6

He went a little farther and fell on His face, and prayed, saying, "O My Father, if it is possible, let this cup pass from me; nevertheless, not as I will, but as You *will*."
Matthew 26:39

Likewise the Spirit also helps in our weaknesses. For we do not know what we should pray for as we ought, but the Spirit Himself makes intercession for us with groanings which cannot be uttered. Now He who searches the hearts knows what the mind of the Spirit *is*, because He makes intercession for the saints according to *the will of* God. Romans 8:26-27

For this reason we also, since the day we heard it, do not cease to pray for you, and to ask that you may be filled with the knowledge of His will in all wisdom and spiritual understanding. Colossians 1:9

Epaphras, who is *one* of you, a bondservant of Christ, greets you, always laboring fervently for you in prayers, that you may stand perfect and complete in all the will of God. Colossians 4:12

Now may the God of peace who brought up our Lord Jesus from the dead, that great Shepherd of the sheep, through the blood of the everlasting covenant, make you complete in every good work to do His will, working in you what is well pleasing in His sight, through Jesus Christ, to whom *be* glory forever and ever. Amen. Hebrews 13:20-21

Now this is the confidence that we have in Him, that if we ask anything according to His will, He hears us. And if we know that He hears us, whatever we ask, we know that we have the petitions that we have asked of Him.
1 John 5:14-15

INSTRUCTIONS REGARDING THE WILL OF GOD

I beseech you therefore, brethren, by the mercies of God, that you present your bodies a living sacrifice, holy, acceptable to God, *which is* your reasonable service. And do not be conformed to this world, but be transformed by the renewing of your mind, that you may prove what *is* that good and acceptable and perfect will of God.
Romans 12:1-2

Therefore do not be unwise, but understand what the will of the Lord *is*. Ephesians 5:17

Bondservants, be obedient to those who are your masters according to the flesh, with fear and trembling, in sincerity of heart, as to Christ; not with eye service, as men-pleasers, but as bondservants of Christ, doing the will of God from the heart. Ephesians 6:5-6

For this is the will of God, your sanctification: that you should abstain from sexual immorality; that each of you should know how to possess his own vessel in sanctification and honor. 1 Thessalonians 4:3-4

Rejoice always, pray without ceasing, in everything give thanks; for this is the will of God in Christ Jesus for you. 1 Thessalonians 5:16-18

For you have need of endurance, so that after you have done the will of God, you may receive the promise. Hebrews 10:36

Come now, you who say, "Today or tomorrow we will go to such and such a city, spend a year there, buy and sell, and make a profit"; whereas you do not know what *will happen* tomorrow. For what *is* your life? It is even a vapor that appears for a little time and then vanishes away. Instead you *ought* to say, "If the Lord wills, we shall live and do this or that." James 4:13-15

Therefore submit yourselves to every ordinance of man for the Lord's sake, whether to the king as supreme, or to governors, as to those who are sent by him for the punishment of evildoers and *for the* praise of those who do good. For this is the will of God, that by doing good you may put to silence the ignorance of foolish men as free, yet not using liberty as a cloak for vice, but as bondservants of

God. Honor all *people*. Love the brotherhood. Fear God. Honor the king. 1Peter 2:13-17

Therefore, since Christ suffered for us in the flesh, arm yourselves also with the same mind, for he who has suffered in the flesh has ceased from sin, that he no longer should live the rest of *his* time in the flesh for the lusts of men, but for the will of God. 1 Peter 4:1-2

Therefore let those who suffer according to the will of God commit their souls *to him* in doing good, as to a faithful Creator. 1 Peter 4:19

TEACHINGS ABOUT THE WILL OF GOD

So Samuel said:
"Has the Lord *as great* delight
in burnt offerings and sacrifices,
as in obeying the voice of the Lord?
Behold, to obey is better than sacrifice,
And to heed than the fat of rams. 1 Samuel 15:22

For I desire mercy and not sacrifice,
and the knowledge
of God more than burnt offerings. Hosea 6:6

He has shown you, O man, what *is* good;
And what does the Lord require of you
But to do justly, to love mercy,
And to walk humbly with your God? Micah 6:8

When Jesus heard *that,* He said to them, "Those who are well have no need of a physician, but those who are sick.

But go and learn what *this* means: 'I desire mercy and not sacrifice.' For I did not come to call the righteous, but sinners, to repentance."
Matthew 9:12-13

And He looked around in a circle at those who sat about Him, and said, "Here are my mother and my brothers! For whoever does the will of God is my brother and My sister and mother." Mark 3:34-35

Moreover, brethren, we make known to you the grace of God bestowed on the churches of Macedonia: that in a great trial of affliction the abundance of their joy and their deep poverty abounded in the riches of their liberality. For I bear witness that according to *their* ability, yes, and beyond *their* ability, *they were* freely willing, imploring us with much urgency that we would receive the gift and the fellowship of the ministering to the saints. And not *only* as we had hoped, but they first gave themselves to the Lord, and *then* to us by the will of God. 2 Corinthians 8:1-5

Previously saying, "Sacrifice and offering, burnt offerings, and *offerings* for sin you did not desire, nor had pleasure *in them*" (which are offered according to the law), then He said, "Behold, I have come to do Your will, O God." He takes away the first that He may establish the second. By that will we have been sanctified through the offering of the body of Jesus Christ once *for all*.
Hebrews 10:8-10

But, beloved, do not forget this one thing, that with the Lord one day *is* as a thousand years, and a thousand years as one day. The Lord is not slack concerning *His* promise, as some count slackness, but is longsuffering toward us, not willing that any should perish but that all should come to repentance. 2 Peter 3:8-9

Praying For Reconciliation

RECONCILIATION WITH GOD

But now in Christ Jesus you who once were far off have been brought near by the blood of Christ. For He Himself is our peace, who has made both one, and has broken down the middle wall of separation, having abolished in His flesh the enmity, *that is,* the law of commandments *contained* in ordinances, so as to create in Himself one new man *from* the two, *thus* making peace, and that He might reconcile them both to God in one body through the cross, thereby putting to death the enmity. And He came and preached peace to you who were afar off and to those who were near. For through Him we both have access by one Spirit to the Father. He is the image of the invisible God, the firstborn over all creation. For by Him all things were created that are in heaven and that are on earth, visible and invisible, whether thrones or dominions or principalities or powers. All things were created through Him and for Him. And He is before all things, and in Him all things consist. And He is the head of the body, the church, who is the beginning, the firstborn from the dead, that in all things He may have the preeminence. For it pleased *the Father that* in Him all the fullness should dwell, and by Him to reconcile all things to Himself, by Him, whether things on earth or things in heaven, having made peace through the blood of His cross. Colossians 1:15–20

For the love of Christ compels us, because we judge thus: that if One died for all, then all died; and He died for all, that those who live should live no longer for themselves, but for Him who died for them and rose again. Therefore, from now on, we regard no one according to the flesh. Even though we have known Christ according to the flesh, yet now we know *Him thus* no longer. Therefore, if anyone *is* in Christ, *he is* a new creation; old things have passed away; behold, all things have become new. Now all things *are* of God, who has reconciled us to Himself through Jesus Christ, and has given us the ministry of reconciliation, that is, that God was in Christ reconciling the world to Himself, not imputing their trespasses to them, and has committed to us the word of reconciliation. Now then, we are ambassadors for Christ, as though God were pleading through us: we implore *you* on Christ's behalf, be reconciled to God. For He made Him who knew no sin *to be* sin for us, that we might become the righteousness of God in Him.
2 Corinthians 5:14–21

Praying For Christ Like
Treatment Of One Another

THE COMMANDMENT TO LOVE ONE ANOTHER

A new commandment I give to you, that you love one another; as I have loved you, that you also love one another. By this all will know that you are my disciples, if you have love for one another. John 13:34–35

Owe no one anything except to love one another, for he who loves another has fulfilled the law. Romans 13:8

Since you have purified your souls in obeying the truth through the Spirit in sincere love of the brethren, love one another fervently with a pure heart. 1 Peter 1:22

For this is the message that you heard from the beginning, that we should love one another. 1 John 3:11

And this is His commandment: that we should believe on the name of His Son Jesus Christ and love one another, as He gave us commandment. 1 John 3:23

Beloved, let us love one another, for love is of God; and everyone who loves is born of God and knows God. 1 John 4:7

Beloved, if God so loved us, we also ought to love one another. No one has seen God at any time. If we love one another, God abides in us, and His love has been perfected in us. 1 John 4:11–12

DEVOTED IN BROTHERLY LOVE

Be kindly affectionate to one another with brotherly love, in honor giving preference to one another. Romans 12:10

LIVING IN HARMONY WITH ONE ANOTHER

Be of the same mind toward one another. Do not set your mind on high things, but associate with the humble. Do not be wise in your own opinion. Romans 12:16

Finally, all *of you be* of one mind, having compassion for one another; love as brothers, *be* tenderhearted, *be* courteous. 1 Peter 3:8

Therefore let us not judge one another anymore, but rather resolve this, not to put a stumbling block or a cause to fall in *our* brother's way. Romans 14:13

Therefore receive one another, just as Christ also received us, to the glory of God. Romans 15:7

Now I plead with you, brethren, by the name of our Lord Jesus Christ, that you all speak the same thing, and *that* there be no divisions among you, but *that* you be perfectly joined together in the same mind and in the same judgment. 1 Corinthians 1:10

For you, brethren, have been called to liberty; only do not *use* liberty as an opportunity for the flesh, but through love serve one another. Galatians 5:13

DO NOT JUDGE

Therefore let us not judge one another anymore, but rather resolve this, not to put a stumbling block or a cause to fall in *our* brother's way. Romans 14:13

ACCEPTING ONE ANOTHER

Therefore receive one another, just as Christ also received us, to the glory of God. Romans 15:7

UNITED IN MIND AND THOUGHT

Now I plead with you, brethren, by the name of our Lord Jesus Christ, that you all speak the same thing, and *that* there be no divisions among you, but *that* you be perfectly joined together in the same mind and in the same judgment. 1 Corinthians 1:10

SERVE ONE ANOTHER

For you, brethren, have been called to liberty; only do not *use* liberty as an opportunity for the flesh, but through love serve one another. Galatians 5:13

BEAR EACH OTHER IN LOVE

With all lowliness and gentleness, with long-suffering, bearing with one another in love. Ephesians 4:2

BE KIND AND COMPASSIONATE

And be kind to one another, tenderhearted, forgiving one another, even as God in Christ forgave you. Ephesians 4:32

SUBMIT TO ONE ANOTHER

Submitting to one another in the fear of God.
Ephesians 5:21

FORGIVE AND BEAR ONE ANOTHER

Therefore, as *the* elect of God, holy and beloved, put on tender mercies, kindness, humility, meekness, long suffering; bearing with one another, and forgiving one another, if anyone has a complaint against another; even as Christ forgave you, so you also *must do*. But above all these things put on love, which is the bond of perfection. Colossians 3:12–14

LIVE IN PEACE

Be at peace among yourselves. 1 Thessalonians 5:13b

ENCOURAGE EACH OTHER

But exhort one another daily, while it is called "Today," lest any of you be hardened through the deceitfulness of sin. Hebrews 3:13

STIMULATING EACH OTHER
TO LOVE AND GOOD WORKS

And let us consider one another in order to stir up love and good works, not forsaking the assembling of ourselves together, as *is* the manner of some, but exhorting *one another,* and so much the more as you see the day approaching. Hebrews 10:24–25

BE HOSPITABLE

Be hospitable to one another without grumbling. As each one has received a gift, minister it to one another, as good stewards of the manifold grace of God. 1 Peter 4:9–10

Praying As Jesus Would

JESUS' PRACTICE IN PRAYER

He Prayed In The Morning

Now in the morning, having risen a long while before daylight, He went out and departed to a solitary place; and there He prayed. Mark 1:35

He Thanked God Before a Meal

Then He commanded the multitudes to sit down on the grass. And He took the five loaves and the two fish, and looking up to heaven, He blessed and broke and gave the loaves to the disciples; and the disciples gave to the multitudes. Matthew 14:19

He Prayed Before Crucial Determinations

Now it came to pass in those days that He went out to the mountain to pray, and continued all night in prayer to God. And when it was day, He called His disciples to *Himself;* and from them He chose twelve whom He also named apostles. Luke 6:12–13

He Prayed For The Faith of Another

And the Lord said, "Simon, Simon! Indeed, Satan has asked for you, that he may sift *you* as wheat. But I have prayed for you, that your faith should not fail; and when you have returned to *me,* strengthen your brethren."
Luke 22:31–32

He Prayed For The Will Of God To Be Done

Then He said to them, "My soul is exceedingly sorrowful, *even* to death. Stay here and watch." He went a little farther, and fell on the ground, and prayed that if it were possible, the hour might pass from Him. And He said, "Abba, Father, all things *are* possible for you. Take this cup away from me; nevertheless, not what I will, but what you *will*." Mark 14:34–36

JESUS' TEACHINGS ON PRAYER

You have heard that it was said, 'You shall love your neighbor and hate your enemy.' But I say to you, love your enemies, bless those who curse you, do good to those who hate you, and pray for those who spitefully use you and persecute you. Matthew 5:43-44

And when you pray, you shall not be like the hypocrites. For they love to pray standing in the synagogues and on the corners of the streets, that they may be seen by men. Assuredly, I say to you, they have their reward. But you, when you pray, go into your room, and when you have shut your door, pray to your Father who *is* in the secret *place;* and your Father who sees in secret will reward you openly. And when you pray, do not use vain repetitions as the heathen *do.* For they think that they will be heard for their many words. Therefore do not be like them. For your Father knows the things you have need of before you ask Him. Matthew 6:5–8

Then He spoke a parable to them, that men always ought to pray and not lose heart, saying: "There was in a certain city a judge who did not fear God nor regard man. Now there was a widow in that city; and she came to him, saying, 'Get justice for me from my adversary.' And he would not for a while; but afterward he said within himself, 'Though I do not fear God nor regard man, yet because this widow troubles me I will avenge her, lest by her continual coming she weary me.'"

Then the Lord said, "Hear what the unjust judge said. And shall God not avenge His own elect who cry out day and night to Him, though He bears long with them? I tell you that He will avenge them speedily. Nevertheless, when the Son of Man comes, will He really find faith on the earth?" Luke 18:1–8

So I say to you, ask, and it will be given to you; seek, and you will find; knock, and it will be opened to you. For everyone who asks receives, and he who seeks finds, and to him who knocks it will be opened. Luke 11:9–10

But when he saw the multitudes, he was moved with compassion for them, because they were weary and scattered, like sheep having no shepherd. Then He said to His disciples, "The harvest truly *is* plentiful, but the laborers *are* few. Therefore pray the Lord of the harvest to send out laborers into His harvest." Matthew 9:36–38

So Jesus answered and said to them, "Assuredly, I say to you, if you have faith and do not doubt, you will not only do what was done to the fig tree, but also if you say to this mountain, 'Be removed and be cast into the sea,' it will be done. And whatever things you ask in prayer, believing, you will receive." Matthew 21:21–22

And whatever you ask in my name, that I will do, that the Father may be glorified in the Son. If you ask anything in my name, I will do *it*. John 14:13–14

You did not choose me, but I chose you and appointed you that you should go and bear fruit, and *that* your fruit should remain, that whatever you ask the Father in My name He may give you. John 15:16

Therefore you now have sorrow; but I will see you again and your heart will rejoice, and your joy no one will take from you. "And in that day you will ask me nothing. Most assuredly, I say to you, whatever you ask the Father in my name He will give you. Until now you have asked nothing in my name. Ask, and you will receive, that your joy may be full." John 16:22–24

If you abide in me, and my words abide in you, you will ask what you desire, and it shall be done for you. John 15:7

FROM JESUS' PRAYER FOUND IN JOHN 17

That the Son would be glorified (vv. 1–5)

Jesus spoke these words, lifted up His eyes to heaven, and said: "Father, the hour has come. Glorify Your Son, that Your Son also may glorify you, as you have given Him authority over all flesh, that He should give eternal life to as many as You have given Him. And this is eternal life, that they may know you, the only true God, and Jesus Christ whom you have sent. I have glorified you on the earth. I have finished the work, which you have given me to do.

And now, O Father, glorify me together with yourself, with the glory, which I had with you before the world was.

That believers would be protected and be unified (vv. 9–11)

"I pray for them. I do not pray for the world but for those whom you have given me, for they are yours. And all Mine are yours, and yours are mine, and I am glorified in them. Now I am no longer in the world, but these are in the world, and I come to you. Holy Father, keep through your name those whom you have given me, that they may be one as we *are*.

That believers would have his joy (v. 13)

But now I come to you, and these things I speak in the world, that they may have my joy fulfilled in themselves.

That believers would be protected from Satan (vv. 14–15)

I have given them your word; and the world has hated them because they are not of the world, just as I am not of the world. I do not pray that you should take them out of the world, but that you should keep them from the evil one.

That believers would be sanctified by the word of God (v. 17)

Sanctify them by your truth. Your word is truth.

That future believers be unified with God the father and the son (vv. 20-23)

"I do not pray for these alone, but also for those who will believe in me through their word; that they all may be one, as you, Father, *are* in me, and I in you; that they also may be one in us, that the world may believe that you sent me. And the glory which you gave me I have given them, that they may be one just as we are one: I in them, and you in me; that they may be made perfect in one, and that the world may know that you have sent me, and have loved them as you have loved me.

That the love of the Father would be in them (v. 26)

And I have declared to them your name, and will declare *it,* that the love with which you loved me may be in them, and I in them."

Worshiping Him In Prayer For His Attributes

HE IS OMNISCIENT

O Lord, You have searched me and known *me.*
You know my sitting down and my rising up;
You understand my thought afar off.
You comprehend my path and my lying down,
And are acquainted with all my ways.
For *there is* not a word on my tongue,
But behold, O Lord, You know it altogether.
You have hedged me behind and before,
And laid your hand upon me.
Such knowledge *is* too wonderful for me;
It is high, I cannot *attain* it. Psalm 139:1–6

HE IS OMNIPRESENT

Where can I go from your Spirit?

Or where can I flee from your presence?
If I ascend into heaven, you *are* there;
If I make my bed in hell, behold, you *are there*.
If I take the wings of the morning,
And dwell in the uttermost parts of the sea,
Even there your hand shall lead me,
And your right hand shall hold me.
If I say, "Surely the darkness shall fall on me,"
Even the night shall be light about me;
Indeed, the darkness shall not hide from you,
But the night shines as the day;
The darkness and the light *are* both alike *to you*.
Psalm 139:7–12

HE IS RIGHTEOUS AND JUST

For I proclaim the name of the Lord:
Ascribe greatness to our God.
He is the Rock, his work *is* perfect;
For all his ways *are* justice,
A God of truth and without injustice;
Righteous and upright *is* He. Deuteronomy 32:3-4

Whom God set forth *as* a propitiation by His blood, through faith, to demonstrate His righteousness, because in His forbearance God had passed over the sins that were previously committed, to demonstrate at the present time His righteousness, that He might be just and the justifier of the one who has faith in Jesus. Romans 3:25–26

HE IS SOVEREIGN

Whatever the Lord pleases he does,

In heaven and in earth,
In the seas and in all deep places. Psalm 135:6

HE IS SUPREME

Indeed heaven and the highest heavens belong to the Lord your God, *also* the earth with all that *is* in it. For the Lord your God *is* God of gods and Lord of lords, the great God, mighty and awesome, who shows no partiality nor takes a bribe. Deuteronomy 10:14, 17

HE IS TRUE

Jesus said to him, "I am the way, the truth, and the life. No one comes to the Father except through me." John 14:6

And this is eternal life, that they may know you, the only true God, and Jesus Christ whom you have sent. John 17:3

HE IS HOLY

In the year that King Uzziah died, I saw the Lord sitting on a throne, high and lifted up, and the train of His *robe* filled the temple. Above it stood seraphim; each one had six wings: with two he covered his face, with two he covered his feet, and with two he flew. And one cried to another and said: "Holy, holy, holy *is* the Lord of hosts; The whole earth *is* full of His glory!" Isaiah 6:1–3

But as He who called you *is* holy, you also be holy in all *your* conduct, because it is written, "Be holy, for I am holy." 1 Peter 1:15–16

HE IS IMMUTABLE

God *is* not a man, that he should lie,
Nor a son of man that he should repent.
Has he said, and will he not do?
Or has He spoken, and will He not make it good?
Numbers 23:19

"For I *am* the Lord, I do not change; therefore you are not consumed, O sons of Jacob." Malachi 3:6

HE IS LOVE

The Lord has appeared of old to me, *saying:*
"Yes, I have loved you with an everlasting love;
Therefore with loving-kindness I have drawn you."
Jeremiah 31:3
Beloved, let us love one another, for love is of God; and everyone who loves is born of God and knows God. He who does not love does not know God, for God is love. In this the love of God was manifested toward us, that God has sent His only begotten Son into the world, that we might live through Him. In this is love, not that we loved God, but that He loved us and sent His Son *to be* the propitiation for our sins. Beloved, if God so loved us, we also ought to love one another. No one has seen God at any time. If we love one another, God abides in us, and His love has been perfected in us. 1 John 4:7–12

HE IS ETERNAL

Before the mountains were brought forth,
Or ever you had formed the earth and the world,

Even from everlasting to everlasting, you *are* God.
Psalm 90:2

Jesus Christ *is* the same yesterday, today, and forever.
Hebrews 13:8

HE IS GRACIOUS

And the Word became flesh and dwelt among us, and we beheld His glory, the glory as of the only begotten of the Father, full of grace and truth. For the law was given through Moses, *but* grace and truth came through Jesus Christ. John 1:14, 17

For by grace you have been saved through faith, and that not of yourselves; *it is* the gift of God, not of works, lest anyone should boast. Ephesians 2:8–9

But when the kindness and the love of God our Savior toward man appeared, not by works of righteousness which we have done, but according to His mercy He saved us, through the washing of regeneration and renewing of the Holy Spirit, whom He poured out on us abundantly through Jesus Christ our Savior, that having been justified by His grace we should become heirs according to the hope of eternal life. Titus 3:4-7

HE IS OMNIPOTENT

Have you not known?
Have you not heard?
The everlasting God, the Lord,
The Creator of the ends of the earth,

Neither faints nor is weary.
His understanding is unsearchable.
He gives power to the weak,
And to *those who have* no might
He increases strength.
Even the youths shall faint and be weary,
And the young men shall utterly fall,
But those who wait on the Lord
Shall renew *their* strength;
They shall mount up with wings like eagles,
They shall run and not be weary,
They shall walk and not faint. Isaiah 40:28–31

Who being the brightness of *His* glory and the express image of His person, and upholding all things by the word of His power, when He had by Himself purged our sins, sat down at the right hand of the Majesty on high. Hebrews 1:3

Worshiping Jesus In Prayer
For Who He Is

JESUS IS OUR HIGH PRIEST

Therefore, in all things he had to be made like *his* brethren, that He might be a merciful and faithful High Priest in things *pertaining* to God, to make propitiation for the sins of the people. For in that He Himself has suffered, being tempted, He is able to aid those who are tempted. Hebrews 2:17–18

Seeing then that we have a great High Priest who has passed through the heavens, Jesus the Son of God, let us

hold fast *our* confession. For we do not have a High Priest who cannot sympathize with our weaknesses, but was in all *points* tempted as *we are, yet* without sin. Let us therefore come boldly to the throne of grace that we may obtain mercy and find grace to help in time of need.
Hebrews 4:14–16

For Christ has not entered the holy places made with hands, *which are* copies of the true, but into heaven itself, now to appear in the presence of God for us; not that He should offer Himself often, as the high priest enters the most holy place every year with blood of another— He then would have had to suffer often since the foundation of the world; but now, once at the end of the ages, He has appeared to put away sin by the sacrifice of Himself. And as it is appointed for men to die once, but after this the judgment, so Christ was offered once to bear the sins of many. To those who eagerly wait for Him He will appear a second time, apart from sin, for salvation. Hebrews 9:24–28

JESUS IS THE LAMB OF GOD

And I looked, and behold, in the midst of the throne and of the four living creatures, and in the midst of the elders, stood a Lamb as though it had been slain, having seven horns and seven eyes, which are the seven Spirits of God sent out into all the earth. Then He came and took the scroll out of the right hand of Him who sat on the throne.
Now when he had taken the scroll, the four living creatures and the twenty-four elders fell down before the Lamb, each having a harp, and golden bowls full of incense, which are the prayers of the saints. And they sang a new song, saying:

"You are worthy to take the scroll,
And to open its seals;
For You were slain,
And have redeemed us to God by Your blood
Out of every tribe and tongue
and people and nation,
And have made us kings and priests to our God;
And we shall reign on the earth."

Then I looked, and I heard the voice of many angels around the throne, the living creatures, and the elders;
and the number of them was ten thousand times ten thousand, and thousands of thousands, saying with a loud voice:

"Worthy is the Lamb who was slain
To receive power and riches and wisdom,
And strength and honor and glory and blessing!"
And every creature, which is in heaven
and on the earth
and under the earth and such as
are in the sea, and all
that are in them, I heard saying:
"Blessing and honor and glory and power
Be to him who sits on the throne,
And to the Lamb, forever and ever!"
Then the four living creatures said,
"Amen!" And the
twenty-four elders fell down
and worshiped Him who
lives forever and ever. Revelation 5:6–14

JESUS AS BONDSERVANT

Yet it shall not be so among you; but whoever desires to become great among you shall be your servant. And whoever of you desires to be first shall be slave of all. For even the Son of Man did not come to be served, but to serve, and to give His life a ransom for many.
Mark 10:43-45

So when he had washed their feet, taken his garments, and sat down again, he said to them, "Do you know what I have done to you? You call me teacher and Lord, and you say well, for *so* I am. If I then, *your* Lord and Teacher, have washed your feet, you also ought to wash one another's feet. For I have given you an example that you should do as I have done to you. Most assuredly, I say to you, a servant is not greater than his master; nor is he who is sent greater than he who sent him. If you know these things, blessed are you if you do them. John 13:12–17

Let this mind be in you which was also in Christ Jesus, who, being in the form of God, did not consider it robbery to be equal with God, but made himself of no reputation, taking the form of a bondservant, *and* coming in the likeness of men. And being found in appearance as a man, He humbled Himself and became obedient to *the point of* death, even the death of the cross. Therefore God also has highly exalted him and given him the name that is above every name, that at the name of Jesus every knee should bow, of those in heaven, and of those on earth, and of those under the earth, and *that* every tongue should confess that

Jesus Christ *is* Lord, to the glory of God the Father.
Philippians 2:5–11

Who has believed our report?
And to whom has the arm
of the Lord been revealed?
For He shall grow up before Him as a tender plant,
And as a root out of dry ground.
He has no form or comeliness;
And when we see Him,
There is no beauty that we should desire Him.
He is despised and rejected by men,
A Man of sorrows and acquainted with grief.
And we hid, as it were, *our* faces from Him;
He was despised, and we did not esteem Him.
Surely He has borne our griefs
And carried our sorrows;
Yet we esteemed Him stricken,
Smitten by God, and afflicted.
But He *was* wounded for our transgressions,
He was bruised for our iniquities;
The chastisement for our peace *was* upon Him,
And by His stripes we are healed.
All we like sheep have gone astray;
We have turned, every one, to his own way;
And the Lord has laid on Him the iniquity of us all.
Isaiah 53:1–6

"The Spirit of the Lord God *is* upon me,
Because the Lord has anointed me
To preach good tidings to the poor;
He has sent me to heal the brokenhearted,
To proclaim liberty to the captives,

And the opening of the prison
to *those who are* bound;
To proclaim the acceptable year of the Lord,
And the day of vengeance of our God;
To comfort all who mourn,
To console those who mourn in Zion,
To give them beauty for ashes,
The oil of joy for mourning,
The garment of praise for the spirit of heaviness;
That they may be called trees of righteousness,
The planting of the Lord, that He may be glorified."
And they shall rebuild the old ruins,
They shall raise up the former desolations,
And they shall repair the ruined cities,
The desolations of many generations.
Strangers shall stand and feed your flocks,
And the sons of the foreigner
Shall be your plowmen and your vinedressers.
Isaiah 61:1-5

JESUS IS THE WORD OF GOD

In the beginning was the Word, and the Word was with God, and the Word was God. He was in the beginning with God. All things were made through Him, and without Him nothing was made that was made. In Him was life, and the life was the light of men. And the light shines in the darkness, and the darkness did not comprehend it.
John 1:1–5

He came to his own, and his own did not receive him. But as many as received him, to them He gave the right to become children of God, to those who believe in his name:

who were born, not of blood, nor of the will of the flesh, nor of the will of man, but of God. And the word became flesh and dwelt among us, and we beheld his glory, the glory as of the only begotten of the Father, full of grace and truth. John 1:11–14

God, who at various times and in various ways spoke in time past to the fathers by the prophets, has in these last days spoken to us by *his* son, whom He has appointed heir of all things, through whom also He made the worlds; who being the brightness of *his* glory and the express image of his person, and upholding all things by the word of his power, when he had by himself purged our sins, sat down at the right hand of the Majesty on high. Hebrews 1:1–3

JESUS IS THE GREAT I AM

Jesus said to them, "Most assuredly, I say to you, before Abraham was, I AM." John 8:58

JESUS IS THE IMAGE OF THE INVISIBLE GOD

He is the image of the invisible God, the firstborn over all creation. For by him all things were created that are in heaven and that are on earth, visible and invisible, whether thrones or dominions or principalities or powers. All things were created through him and for him. And he is before all things, and in him all things consist. And he is the head of the body, the church, who is the beginning, the firstborn from the dead, that in all things he may have the preeminence. For it pleased *the Father that* in him all the fullness should dwell, and by him to reconcile all things to Himself, by him, whether things on earth or things in

heaven, having made peace through the blood of His cross. And you, who once were alienated and enemies in your mind by wicked works, yet now he has reconciled in the body of his flesh through death, to present you holy, and blameless, and above reproach in his sight.
Colossians 1:15-22

Select scriptures and notes ...

_____

_____

_____

_____

_____

_____

_____

_____

_____

_____

_____

_____

_____

_____

_____

_____

_____

_____

_____

Chapter 8

BIBLICAL PROMISES
FOR PRAYING WITH YOUR SPOUSE

God Has Given Us The Victory

Behold, I am with you and will keep you wherever you go, and will bring you back to this land; for I will not leave you until I have done what I have spoken to you.
Genesis 28:15

And Moses said to the people, "Fear not. Stand still, and see the salvation of the Lord, which He will accomplish for you today. For the Egyptians whom you see today, you shall see again no more forever. The Lord will fight for you, and you shall hold your peace."
Exodus 14:13-14

"For I will cast out the nations before you and enlarge your borders;" Exodus 34:24a

I am the Lord your God, who brought you out of the land of Egypt, that you should not be their slaves; I have broken the bands of your yoke and made you go upright. Leviticus 26:13

"Now it shall come to pass, if you diligently obey the voice of the Lord your God, to observe carefully all His commandments which I command you today, that the Lord your God will set you high above all nations of the earth."
"And the Lord will make you the head and not the tail; you shall be above only, and not be beneath, if you heed the commandments of the Lord your God, which I command you today, and are careful to observe them and to do them." Deuteronomy 28:1,13

The eternal God is your refuge, and underneath are the everlasting arms; He shall thrust out the enemy from before you; and will say, "Destroy them!" Deuteronomy 33:27

"Have not I commanded you? Be strong and of good courage; do not be afraid, nor be dismayed, for the Lord your God is with you wherever you go." Joshua 1:9

"Come near, put your feet on the necks of these kings."... Then Joshua said to them, "Fear not, nor be dismayed; be strong and of good courage, for thus the Lord will do to all your enemies against whom you fight." Joshua 10:24b, 25

The Lord is my light and my salvation; whom shall I fear? The Lord is the strength of my life; of whom shall I be afraid? When the wicked, even my enemies and my foes, came upon me to eat up my flesh, they stumbled and fell. Psalm 27:1-2

For they did not gain possession of the land by their own sword, nor did their own arm save them; but it was Your right hand, Your arm, and the light of Your countenance, because You favored them. Psalm 44:3

Destroy, Oh Lord, and divide their tongues, for I have seen violence and strife in the city. Psalm 55:9

When I cry unto You, then shall my enemies turn back: this I know; for God is for me. Psalm 56:9

Through God we shall do valiantly: for He it is that shall tread down our enemies. Psalm 60:12

God Who keeps our soul among the living, and does not allow our feet to be moved. Psalm 66:9

I shall not die, but live, and declare the works of the Lord. Psalm 118:17

For the rod of the wicked shall not rest upon the lot of the righteous. Psalm 125:3

Though I walk in the midst of trouble, you will revive me; You will stretch out Your hand against the wrath of my enemies, and Your right hand will save me. Psalm 138:7

Fear not, for I am with you; be not dismayed, for I am your God. I will strengthen you, yes, I will help you, I will uphold you with the right hand of my righteousness.
Isaiah 41:10

"No weapon formed against you shall prosper, and every tongue which rises against you in judgment you shall condemn. This is the heritage of the servants of the Lord, and their righteousness is from me," says the Lord.
Isaiah 54:17

But the Lord is with me as a mighty, terrible one. Therefore my persecutors shall stumble, and they shall not prevail. They will be greatly ashamed, for they shall not prosper. Their everlasting confusion shall never be forgotten. Jeremiah 20:11

"But I will deliver you in that day," says the Lord, "and you shall not be given into the hand of the men of whom you are afraid. For I will surely deliver you, and you shall not fall by the sword; but your life shall be as a prize to you, because you have put your trust in me," says the Lord. Jeremiah 39:17-18

Sing, O daughter of Zion! Shout, O Israel! Be glad and rejoice with all your heart, O daughter of Jerusalem. The Lord has taken away your judgments; He has cast out your enemy. The King of Israel, the Lord, is in your midst, you shall not see evil any more. Zephaniah 3:14 -15

For if by the one man's offense death reigned through the one, much more those who receive abundance of grace and of the gift of righteousness will reign in life through the One, Jesus Christ. Romans 5:17

But thanks be to God, who gives us the victory through our Lord Jesus Christ. Therefore, my beloved brethren, be steadfast, immovable, always abounding in the work of the Lord, knowing that your labor is not in vain in the Lord. 1 Corinthians 15:57-58

Now thanks be to God who always causes us to triumph in Christ, and through us shows the savor of His knowledge in every place. 2 Corinthians 2:14

But the Lord is faithful, who shall establish you and keep you from evil. 2 Thessalonians 3:3

But the Lord stood with me and strengthened me; that by me the preaching might be fully known, and that all the Gentiles might hear: and I was delivered out of the mouth of the lion. And the Lord shall deliver me from every evil work and preserve me unto His heavenly kingdom. 2 Timothy 4:17-18

Salvation of The Family

For I know him, that he will command his children and his household after him, and they shall keep the way of the Lord, to do justice and judgment; that the Lord may bring upon Abraham that which He has spoken of him. Genesis 18:19

For the Lord your God has chosen him out of all your tribes to stand to minister in the name of the Lord, him and his sons forever. Deuteronomy 18:5

And the Lord your God will circumcise your heart and the heart of your seed, to love the Lord your God with all your heart and with all your soul, that you may live. Deuteronomy 30:6

And his seed is blessed. Psalm 37:26b

Let your work appear to your servants, and your glory to their children. Psalm 90:16

The children of Your servants shall continue, and their seed shall be established before You. Psalm 102:28

But the mercy of the Lord is from everlasting to everlasting upon them that fear Him, and His righteousness to children's children. Psalm 103:17

Blessed is the man that fears the Lord that delights greatly in His commandments. His seed shall be mighty upon the earth: the generation of the upright shall be blessed. Psalm 112:1-2

The Lord shall increase you more and more, you and your children. You are blessed of the Lord, which made heaven and earth. Psalm 115:14-15

Your wife shall be as a fruitful vine in the very heart of your house, your children like olive plants all around your table. Behold that thus shall the man be blessed that fears the Lord. Psalm 128:3-4

Rid me, and deliver me from the hand of strange children, whose mouth speaks vanity, and their right hand is a right hand of falsehood: that our sons may be as plants grown up in their youth; that our daughters may be as corner stones polished after the similitude of a palace.
Psalm 144:11-12

For He has strengthened the bars of your gates; He has blessed your children within you. He makes peace in your borders, and fills you with the finest of the wheat.
Psalm 147:13-14

But the Lord blesses the habitation of the just.
Proverbs 3:33b

Though hand join in hand, the wicked shall not be unpunished; but the seed of the righteous shall be delivered.
Proverbs 11:21

In the fear of the Lord there is strong confidence, and his children shall have a place of refuge. Proverbs 14:26

For I will pour water on him that is thirsty, and floods upon the dry ground; I will pour My Spirit on your seed and My blessing upon your offspring; They will spring up among the grass like willows by the watercourses. One shall say, "I am the Lord's"; another shall call himself by the name of Jacob; and shall write with his hand, to the Lord, and surname himself by the name of Israel. Isaiah 44:3-5

But thus says the Lord: "Even the captives of the mighty shall be taken away, and the prey of the terrible shall be delivered; for I will contend with him who contends with you, and I will save your children." Isaiah 49:25

All your children shall be taught by the Lord, and great shall be the peace of your children. In righteousness you shall be established; you shall be far from oppression, for you shall not fear, and from terror, for it shall not come near you. Isaiah 54:13-14

"As for Me," says the Lord, "this is my covenant with them: my Spirit that is upon you, and my words which I have put in your mouth, shall not depart out of your mouth, nor out of the mouth of your seed, nor out of the mouth of your seed's seed, from this time and forevermore," says the Lord. Isaiah 59:21

They shall not labor in vain, nor bring forth children for trouble; for they are the seed of the blessed of the Lord, and their offspring with them. Isaiah 65:23

Their children also shall be as before, and their congregation shall be established before me; and I will punish all who oppress them. Jeremiah 30:20

Thus says the Lord: "Refrain your voice from weeping, and your eyes from tears; for your work shall be rewarded," says the Lord, "and they shall come again from the land of the enemy. There is hope in your future" says the Lord, "that your children shall come again to their own border." Jeremiah 31:16-17

But do not fear, O My servant Jacob, and do not be dismayed O Israel! For behold I will save you from afar, and your seed from the land of their captivity; Jacob shall return, be in rest and be at ease; no-one shall make him afraid. Jeremiah 46:27

As for you also, by the blood of your covenant I have sent forth your prisoners out of the pit wherein is no water. Zechariah 9:11

Believe on the Lord Jesus Christ and you shall be saved, you and your household. Acts 16:31

For the unbelieving husband is sanctified by the wife, and the unbelieving wife is sanctified by the husband; otherwise your children would be unclean, but now they are holy. 1 Corinthians 7:14

To Cast Out Fear

Fear not, Abram: I am your shield, and your exceeding great reward. Genesis 15:1

Peace be to you, fear not: your God, and the God of your father, has given you treasure in your sacks. Genesis 43:23

Fear you not, stand still, and see the salvation of the Lord, which He will show to you today: for the Egyptians whom you have seen today, you shall see them again no more forever. The Lord shall fight for you, and you shall hold your peace. Exodus 14:13,14

Only rebel not you against the Lord, neither fear you the people of the land; for they are bread for us: their defense is departed from them, and the Lord is with us: fear them not. Numbers 14:9

Have not I commanded you? Be strong and of a good courage; be not afraid, neither be dismayed: for the Lord your God is with you where ever you go. Joshua 1:9

Be strong and of good courage and do it: fear not, nor be dismayed: for the Lord God, even my God, will be with you; he will not fail you, nor forsake you, until you have finished all the work for the service of the house of the Lord. 1Chronicles 28:20

Yes, though I walk through the valley of the shadow of death, I will fear no evil: for you are with me; your rod and your staff comfort me. Psalm 23:4

The Lord is my light and my salvation; whom shall I fear? The Lord is the strength of my life; of whom shall I be afraid? When the wicked, even my enemies and my foes, came upon me to eat up my flesh, they stumbled and fell. Psalm 27:1-2

I sought the Lord, and He heard me, and delivered me from all my fears. Psalm 34:4

God is our refuge and strength, a very present help in trouble. Therefore we will not fear, though the earth be removed, and though the mountains be carried into the sea. Psalm 46:1-2

Say to them that are afraid, "Be strong, fear not: behold, your God will come with vengeance, even God with a recompense; He will come and save you. Isaiah 35:4

Fear not; for I am with you: be not dismayed; for I am your God: I will strengthen you; yes, I will help you; Yes, I will uphold you with the right hand of my righteousness. Isaiah 41:10

Fear not: for 1 have redeemed you, I have called you by your name; you are mine. When you pass through the waters, I will be with you; and through the rivers, they shall not overflow you: when you walk through the fire, you shall not be burned; neither shall the flame kindle upon you. For I am the Lord your God, the Holy One of Israel, your Savior. Isaiah 43:1-3

Fear not, neither be afraid: have not I told you from that time, and have declared it? You are even My witnesses. Is there a God beside Me? Yes, there is no God; I know not any. Isaiah 44:8

No weapon that is formed against you shall prosper; and every tongue that shall rise against you in judgment you shall condemn. This is the heritage of the servants of the Lord, and their righteousness is of Me, says the Lord. Isaiah 54:17

According to the word that I covenanted with you when you came out of Egypt, so my Spirit remains among you: fear you not. Haggai 2:5

Therefore do not worry about tomorrow, for tomorrow will worry about its own things. Sufficient for the day is its own trouble. Matthew 6:34

Behold I give to you power to tread on serpents and scorpions and over all the power of the enemy: and nothing shall by any means hurt you. Luke 10:19

But He said to them, "It is I, do not be afraid." John 6:20

Peace I leave with you, my peace I give to you: not as the world gives, give I to you. Let not your heart be troubled, neither let it be afraid. John 14:27

For you have not received the spirit of bondage again to fear; but you have received the Spirit of adoption, by whom we cry, "Abba, Father." Romans 8:15

For God has not given us the spirit of fear; but of power, and of love and of a sound mind. 2 Timothy 1:7

That through death He might destroy him that had the power of death, that is, the devil; and deliver them who through fear of death were all their lifetime subject to bondage. Hebrews 2:14b, 15

For He has said, "I will never leave you nor forsake you." So that we may boldly say, "The Lord is my helper, and I will not fear what man shall do to me."
Hebrews 13:5b, 6

You are of God, little children, and have overcome them: because greater is He that is in you, than he that is in the world. 1John 4:4

Forgiveness In Jesus' Name

Bless the Lord, O my soul, and forget not all His benefits: who forgives all your iniquities; who heals all your diseases. As far as the east is from the west, so far has He removed our transgressions from us. Psalm 103:2,3,12

O give thanks to the Lord, for He is good: for His mercy endures forever. Let the redeemed of the Lord say so, whom He has redeemed from the hand of the enemy.
Psalm 107:1-2

Come now, and let us reason together, says the Lord: though your sins be as scarlet, they shall be as white as snow; though they be red like crimson, they shall be as wool. Isaiah 1:18

I, even I, am He that blots out your transgressions for mine own sake, and will not remember your sins.
Isaiah 43:25

But He was wounded for our transgressions, He was bruised for our iniquities: the chastisement of our peace was upon Him; and with His stripes we are healed. All we like sheep have gone astray; we have turned everyone to his own way; and the Lord has laid on Him the iniquity of us all.
Isaiah 53:5-6

For I will forgive their iniquity, and I will remember their sin no more. Jeremiah 31:34

And I will cleanse them from all their iniquity, whereby they have sinned against me; and I will pardon their iniquities, whereby they have sinned, and whereby they transgressed against me. Jeremiah 33:8

To the Lord our God belong mercies and forgiveness, though we have rebelled against Him. Daniel 9:9

And she shall bring forth a Son, and You shall call His name JESUS: for He shall save His people from their sins. Matthew 1:21

For this is my blood of the New Testament, which is shed for many for the remission of sins. Matthew 26:28

The next day John sees Jesus coming to him, and says, "Behold the Lamb of God, which takes away the sin of the world." John 1:29

Being justified freely by His grace through the redemption that is in Christ Jesus: whom God has set forth to be a propitiation through faith in His blood, to declare His righteousness for the remission of sins that are past, through the forbearance of God. Romans 3:24-25

But God commends His love towards us, in that, while we were yet sinners, Christ died for us. Much more then, being now justified by His blood, we shall be saved from wrath through Him. Romans 5:8-9

For I delivered to you first of all that which I also received, how that Christ died for our sins according to the scriptures. 1 Corinthians 15:3

In whom we have redemption through His blood, the forgiveness of sins, according to the riches of His grace. Ephesians 1:7

But now in Christ Jesus you who sometimes were far off are made nigh by the blood of Christ. Ephesians 2:13

And be kind one to another, tenderhearted, forgiving one another, even as God for Christ's sake has forgiven you. Ephesians 4:32

In whom we have redemption through His blood, even the forgiveness of sins. Colossians 1:14

This is a faithful saying, and worthy of all acceptation, that Christ Jesus came into the world to save sinners; of whom I am chief. 1Timothy 1:15

How much more shall the blood of Christ, who through the eternal Spirit offered Himself without spot to God, purge your conscience from dead works to serve the living God? Hebrews 9:14

Who his own self bare our sins in his own body on the tree, that we, being dead to sins, should live to righteousness: by Whose stripes you were healed. 1Peter 2:24

For Christ also has once suffered for sins, the just for the unjust, that He might bring us to God, being put to death in the flesh, but quickened by the Spirit. 1Peter 3:18

But if we walk in the light, as he is in the light, we have fellowship one with another, and the blood of Jesus Christ His Son cleanses us from all sin.
If we confess our sins, He is faithful and just to forgive us our sins, and to cleanse us from all unrighteousness.
1John 1:7,9

To him that loved us, and washed us from our sins in his own blood. Revelation 1:5

God Will Answer

Behold the fowls of the air: for they sow not, neither do they reap, nor gather into barns; yet your heavenly Father feeds them. Are you not much better than they?
Matthew 6:26

Ask and it shall be given you; seek and you shall find; knock and it shall be opened to you. For every one that asks receives; and he that seeks finds; and to him that knocks it shall be opened. Matthew 7:7-8
If you then, being evil, know how to give good gifts to your children, how much more shall your Father who is in heaven give good things to them that ask him?
Matthew 7:11

Jesus said, "For truly I say unto you, if you have faith as a grain of mustard seed, you shall say to this mountain remove hence to yonder place; and it shall be moved; and nothing shall be impossible to you." Matthew 17:20

If two of you shall agree on earth as touching anything that they shall ask, it shall be done for them of my Father who is in heaven. For where two or three are gathered together in my name, there am I in the midst of them. Matthew 18:19-20

And all things, whatsoever you shall ask in prayer, believing, you shall receive. Matthew 21:22

Whosoever shall say unto this mountain be thou removed and be cast into the sea; and shall not doubt in his heart, but shall believe that those things, which he says, shall come to pass: he shall have whatsoever he says. Mark 11:23-24

And I say to you, "Ask and it shall be given you; seek and you shall find; knock and it shall be opened to you. For everyone that asks receives; and he that seeks finds; and to him that knocks it shall be opened." Luke 11:9-10

If you then being evil, know how to give good gifts to your children: how much more shall your heavenly Father give the Holy Spirit to them that asks Him? Luke 11:13

Jesus said, "I am the bread of life: he that comes to me shall never hunger; and he that believeth on me shall never thirst." John 6:35

Whatsoever you shall ask in my name, that will I do, that the Father may be glorified in the son. If you shall ask anything in my name, I will do it. John 14:13-14

If you abide in me, and my words abide in you, you will ask what you will and it shall be done for you. John 15:7

That whatsoever you shall ask of the Father in my name he may give it to you. John 15:16b

And in that day you shall ask me nothing. Truly, truly I say to you, "Whatsoever you shall ask the Father in my name, he will give it to you. Hitherto have you asked nothing in my name: ask and you shall receive, that your joy may be full." John 16:23-24

He that spared not his own Son, but delivered Him up for us all, how shall He not with Him also freely give us all things. Romans 8:32

For whosoever shall call upon the Name of the Lord shall be saved. Romans 10:13

But my God shall supply all your need according to His riches in glory by Christ Jesus. Philippians 4:19

But without faith it is impossible to please him; for he that comes to God, must believe that he is, and that he is a rewarder of them that diligently seek him. Hebrews 11:6

If any of you lack wisdom, let him ask of God, that gives to all men liberally and reproves not; and it shall be given him. But let him ask in faith, nothing wavering. For he that wavers is like the wave of the sea driven with the wind and tossed. James 1:5-8

And whatsoever we ask, we receive of him, because we keep his commandments and do those things that are pleasing in his sight. And this is his commandment, that we should believe in his son Jesus Christ, and love one another, as he gave us commandment. 1John 3:22-23

This is the confidence that we have in Him, that if we ask anything according to His will, He hears us: and if we know that He hears us, whatsoever we ask, we know, that we have the petitions that we desired of Him. 1John 5:14-15

His Strength In Us

And as your days, so shall your strength be. Deuteronomy 33:25b

Have not I commanded? Be strong and of a good courage, be not afraid, neither be dismayed: for the Lord your God is with you wherever you go. Joshua 1:9

Be strong therefore, and let not your hands be weak: for your work shall be rewarded. 2 Chronicles 15:7

For the joy of the Lord is your strength. Nehemiah 8:10

It is God that girds me with strength, and makes my way perfect. Psalm 18:32

The Lord is my light and my salvation; whom shall I fear? The Lord is the strength of my life; of whom shall I be afraid? Psalm 27:1

Lord, by your favor you have made my mountain to stand strong. Psalm 30: 7

God is our refuge and our strength, a very present help in trouble. Psalm 46:1

Your God has commanded your strength: strengthen, O God, that which you have wrought for us. The God of Israel is He that gives strength and power to his people.
Psalm 68:28,35

I will go in the strength of the Lord God. Psalm 71:16a

My flesh and my heart fails: but God is the strength of my heart, and my portion forever. Psalm 73:26

The Lord is my strength and song and is become my salvation. Psalm 118:14

For He has strengthened the bars of your gates; He has blessed your children within you. Psalm 147:13

In returning and rest shall you be saved; in quietness and in confidence shall be your strength. Isaiah 30:15

He gives power to the faint; and to them that have no might He increases strength. But they that wait upon the Lord shall renew their strength they shall mount up with wings as eagles; they shall run and not be weary; and they shall walk and not faint. Isaiah 40:29, 31

Fear not; for I am with you: be not dismayed; for I am your God: I will strengthen you; yes, I will help you; yes, I will uphold you with the right hand of my righteousness. Isaiah 41:10

My God shall be my strength. Isaiah 49:5b

Let the weak say, I am strong. Joel 3:10

The Lord God is my strength. Habakkuk 3:19

Be strong, all you people of the land, and work: for I am with you, says the Lord of Hosts. Not by might, or by power, but by My Spirit, says the Lord of Hosts. Haggai 2:4b

Not by might, or by power, but by my Spirit, says the Lord of hosts. Zechariah 4:6

And his name through faith in his name has made this man strong. Acts 3:16

He staggered not at the promise of God through unbelief; but was strong in faith, giving glory to God. Romans 4:20

Watch you, stand fast in the faith, quit you like men, be strong. 1 Corinthians 16:13

For though we walk in the flesh, we do not war according to the flesh. For the weapons of our warfare are not carnal but mighty in God for pulling down strongholds, casting down arguments and every high thing that exalts itself against the knowledge of God, bringing every thought into captivity to the obedience of Christ.
2 Corinthians 10:3-5

My grace is sufficient for you: for my strength is made perfect in weakness... for when I am weak, then am I strong.
2 Corinthians 12:9-10

That He would grant you, according to the riches of His glory, to be strengthened with might by His Spirit in the inner man. Ephesians 3:16

Finally, my brethren, be strong in the Lord, and in the power of His might. Ephesians 6:10

I can do all things through Christ who strengthens me. Philippians 4:13

Strengthened with all might, according to His glorious power, unto all patience and longsuffering with joyfulness. Colossians 1:11

You, therefore, my son, be strong in the grace that is in Christ Jesus. 2 Timothy 2:1

Notwithstanding the Lord stood with me, and strengthened me. 2 Timothy 4:17

Who through faith subdued kingdoms, wrought righteousness, obtained promises, stopped the mouths of lions, quenched the violence of fire, escaped the edge of the sword, out of weakness were made strong, waxed valiant in fight. Hebrews 11:33-34

But the God of all grace, who has called us unto His eternal glory by Christ Jesus, after that you have suffered a while, make you perfect, establish, strengthen, settle you. 1Peter 5:10

I have written to you, young men, because you are strong, and the word of God abides in you, and you have overcome the wicked one. 1John 2:14b

And I heard a loud voice saying in heaven, Now is come salvation, and strength, and the kingdom of our God, and the power of His Christ: for the accuser of our brethren is cast down, which accused them before our God day and night. Revelation 12:10

The Calling to Serve Others

I the Lord have called you in righteousness, and will hold your hand, and will keep you, and give you for a covenant of the people, for a light of the Gentiles; to open the blind eyes, to bring out the prisoners from the prison, and them that sit in darkness out of the prison house. I am the Lord: that is my name: and my glory will I not give to another, neither my praise to graven images. Behold the former things are come to pass, and new things do I declare: before they spring forth I tell you of them. Isaiah 42:6-9

Fear not, neither be afraid: have not I told you from that time, and have declared it? You are my witnesses. Is there a God beside me? Yes, there is no God; I know not any. Isaiah 44:8

And He has made my mouth like a sharp sword: in the shadow of His hand has He hidden me, and made me a polished shaft; in His quiver has He hidden me. Isaiah 49:2

The Lord God has given me the tongue of the learned, that I should know how to speak a word in season to him that is weary. He wakens morning by morning; he wakens my ear to hear as the learned. Isaiah 50:4

And I have put my words in your mouth, and I have covered you in the shadow of my hand, that I may plant the heavens, and lay the foundations of the earth, and say to Zion, you are my people. Isaiah 51:16

But seek you first the kingdom of God, and his righteousness; and all these things shall be added to you. Matthew 6:33

But go rather to the lost sheep of the house of Israel. And as you go, preach, saying, "The kingdom of heaven is at hand. Heal the sick, cleanse the lepers, raise the dead, cast out devils: freely you have received, freely give.

But when they deliver you up, take no thought how or what you shall speak: for it shall be given you in that same hour what you shall speak. For it is not you that speak, but the Spirit of your Father which speaks in you. Matthew 10:6-8,19-20

And the King shall answer and say to them, truly I say to you, inasmuch as you have done it to one of the least of these my brethren, you have done it to me. Matthew 25:40

And Jesus came and spoke to them saying, "All power is given to me in heaven and in earth. Go therefore, and teach all nations, baptizing them in the Name of the Father, and of the Son, and of the Holy Spirit: teaching them to observe all things whatsoever I have commanded you: and, lo, I am with you always, even to the end of the world. Amen." Matthew 28:18-20

And you shall love the Lord your God with all your heart, and with all your soul, and with all your mind, and with all strength: this is the first commandant. And the second is like, namely this; you shall love your neighbor as yourself. Mark 12:30-31

And He called his ten servants, and delivered them ten pounds, and said to them, "Occupy until I come." Luke 19:13

If any man thirst, let him come to me, and drink. He that believes me, as the scripture has said, out of his belly shall flow rivers of living water. John 7:37-38

You have not chosen me, but I have chosen you, and ordained you, that you should go and bring forth fruit and that your fruit should remain. John 15:16

But you shall receive power, after the Holy Spirit has come upon you: and you shall be my witnesses .... to the end of earth. Acts 1:8

God has made us able ministers of the New Testament: not of the letter but of the Spirit.....the Spirit gives life. 2 Corinthians 3:6

By love serve one another. Galatians 5:13b

The Lord has made me a minister of the gospel, according to the gift of the grace of God given to me by the effectual working of His power. Ephesians 3:7

By Him therefore let us offer the sacrifice of praise to God continually, that is the fruit of our lips giving thanks to His Name. But do not forget to do good and fellowship: for with such sacrifices God is well pleased. Hebrews 13:15-16

Visit the fatherless and widows in their affliction. James 1:27b

As every man has received the gift, even so minister the same one to another, as good stewards of the manifold grace of God. 1Peter 4:10

The Joy of The Lord

For the joy of the Lord is your strength. Nehemiah 8:10b

But let all those that put their trust in you rejoice: let them ever shout for joy, because you defend them: let them also that love your name be joyful in you. Psalm 5:11

You will show me the path of life: in your presence is fullness of joy; at your right hand there are pleasures for evermore. Psalm 16:11

But you are holy, O You that inhabits the praises of Israel. Psalm 22:3

Weeping may endure for a night, but joy comes in the morning. Psalm 30:5

I will bless the Lord at all times: His praise shall continually be in my mouth. My soul shall make her boast in the Lord: the humble shall hear and be glad. Psalm 34:1,2

And my soul shall be joyful in the Lord: it shall rejoice in His salvation. Psalm 35:9

Let all those that seek you rejoice and be glad in You: let such as love Your salvation say continually, The Lord be magnified. Psalm 40:16

I will praise you, O Lord my God, with all my heart: and I will glorify your name forevermore. Psalm 86:12

Blessed are the people that know the joyful sound: they shall walk, O Lord, in the light of your countenance. In Your name shall they rejoice all the day: and in your righteousness shall they be exalted. For you are the glory of their strength: and in Your favor our horn shall be exalted. For the Lord is our defense; and the Holy One of Israel is our king. Psalm 89:15-18

Go your way, eat your bread with joy, and drink your wine with a merry heart; for God now accepts your works. Ecclesiastes 9:7

Behold God is my salvation; I will trust, and not be afraid: for the Lord Jehovah is my strength and my song; He also is become my salvation. Therefore with joy shall you draw water out of the wells of salvation.

Sing to the Lord; for He has done excellent things: this is known in all the earth. Cry out and shout, you inhabitant of Zion: for great is the Holy One of Israel in the midst of you. Isaiah 12:2-3, 5-6

For you shall go out with joy, and be led forth with peace: the mountains and the hills shall break forth before you into singing, and all the trees of the field shall clap their hands. Isaiah 55:12

To appoint to them that mourn in Zion, to give to them beauty for ashes, the oil of joy for mourning, the garment of praise for the spirit of heaviness: that they might be called trees of righteousness, the planting of the Lord, that He might be glorified. Isaiah 61:3

I will greatly rejoice in the Lord, my soul shall be joyful in my God; for He has clothed me with the garments of salvation, He has covered me with the robe of righteousness, as a bridegroom decks Himself with ornaments, and as a bride adorns herself with jewels. Isaiah 61:10

Your words were found, and I did eat them; and your word was unto me the joy and rejoicing of my heart: for I am called by your name, O Lord God of Hosts.
Jeremiah 15:16

Although the fig tree shall not blossom, neither shall fruit be in the vines; the labor of the olive shall fail, and the fields shall yield no meat; the flock shall be cut off from the fold, and there shall be no herd in the stalls: Yet I will rejoice in the Lord, I will joy in the God of my salvation.
Habakkuk 3:17-18

Sing, O daughter of Zion; shout, O Israel; be glad and rejoice with all the heart, O daughter of Jerusalem. The Lord has taken away your judgments, He has cast out your enemy: the king of Israel, even the Lord, is in the midst of you: you shall not see evil anymore. Zephaniah 3:14-15

Rejoice greatly, O daughter of Zion; shout O daughter of Jerusalem: behold, your King comes to you: He is just, and having salvation. Zechariah 9:9

Blessed are you, when men shall revile you..... Rejoice, and be exceeding glad: for great is your reward in heaven. Matthew 5:11-12

These things have I spoken to you, that my joy might remain in you, and that your joy might be full. John 15:11

For the kingdom of God is not meat and drink; but righteousness and peace, and joy in the Holy Ghost. Romans 14:17

But the fruit of the Spirit is love, joy, peace...
Galatians 5:22

Be filled with the Spirit. Speaking to yourselves in psalms and hymns and spiritual songs, singing and making melody in your heart to the Lord.
Ephesians 5:18-19

Rejoice in the Lord always: and again I say, rejoice.
Philippians 4:4

My brethren, count it all joy when you fall into diverse temptations. James 1:2

Let us be glad and rejoice, and give honor to Him: for the marriage of the Lamb is come, and His wife has made herself ready. Revelation 19:7

Select scriptures and notes …

_____

_____

_____

_____

_____

_____

_____

_____

_____

_____

_____

_____

_____

_____

_____

_____

_____

_____

_____

_____

_____

_____

_____

Conclusion

FINAL WORDS

Jesus himself extends this invitation and promise; "Again I say to you that if two of you agree on earth concerning anything that they ask, it will be done for them by my Father in heaven. For where two or three are gathered together in my name, I am there in the midst of them." (Matthew 18:19-20)

Continue to ask in accordance with God's will, claiming his promises through prayer with your spouse. Persist in prayer because there is great reward for those who do. God's attributes and love far transcend any alternate source we might turn to for help. He, this all-knowing and powerful God, invites us to agree and persist in prayer. So, do. Agree in prayer. Persevere in this discipline. Don't give up! Ask, seek and knock. "Ask, and *it will be given to you*; seek, and *you will find*; knock, and *it will be opened to you*. For everyone who asks *receives*, and he who seeks *finds*, and to him who knocks *it will be opened*." (Matthew

7:7-8) God's answer will come. God is always right on time.

Rejoice in the fact that only two are necessary to invite God's presence and move his hand in a mighty way. Yes! The power of united prayer with your spouse is insuppressible. This power can be unleashed for your life, your marriage, your family and your highest aspirations for the glory of God and the expansion of his kingdom.

ACKNOWLEDGMENTS

To Misael - Thank you for being such an amazing husband. Thank you for playing with the kids and feeding them as I typed away at the computer writing this book. Thank you for cleaning, cooking and rolling up your sleeves to do just about anything necessary to assist me in my journey. I love you more today than the day I said, 'I do'. You are God's gift to me. Thank you for being the spiritual leader of our household and for each and every moment we have enjoyed speaking with God together. Your faith has strengthened mine and your vision has given me hope and direction. I cannot wait to see what God will do next through us for His glory.

To Jaylee – You are such a sweet and bright little girl. Thank you for allowing me to cuddle and talk to you as you sat in my lap while I worked on the contents of this book. You inspire me to be the most Christ like mommy I can be because I know you follow my example. Thank you, too, for every moment we have talked to God together. I love our time of prayer every morning. It gives me strength to embrace each day. I pray this book will be a resource to you when you grow up and come before God with your husband. I sure do love you, my princess!

To Ethan – Thank you, buddy, for being such a sweet boy. You have been so patient with me as I typed 'one last thought' before I put you on the potty, handed you your juice or threw you the ball so you could bat it. Thank you for being content with my arm wrapped around you as I busily typed away with my other hand. You, too, inspire me to be the best mommy I can be. Your smile brightens up my day. I hope this book will assist you when grow up and come together to pray with your wife. I love you with all my heart!

To Mom and Dad - Thank you for cooking for my family and me many a time so that I could take care of this book and so many other things. Thank you for taking care of Ethan and for holding down the fort when Misael and I are gone. Thank you for the faith you instilled in me at a very young age. Thank you for lovingly and patiently raising me meeting all of my needs, including putting a roof over my head. I am now privileged to put a roof over yours. Thank you for everything you continue to do for me on a daily basis.

To God – Thank you for speaking to my heart the weekend of Feb. 27-28, 2015 and gifting me with the strong desire to write to assist married couples in their spiritual growth and relational journey. Thank you for letting me know that it is my prime time to write because you have already given me what writing for this purpose takes. You gave me persistence, knowledge and strength as you wrote this book through me. Thank you for always keeping your promises and for your constant direction in my life. I marvel at your faithfulness! I can't wait to see what you will do next in me for your glory. Your will is my delight!

Made in the USA
San Bernardino, CA
17 November 2019